Derby. The Cathedral of All Saints, the principal parish church of the town until it was raised to cathedral status in 1927. The west tower dates from the early sixteenth century, the nave (designed by James Gibbs) was built between 1723 and 1725 and the east end dates from 1972.

Shire County Guide 6
DERBYSHIRE
and the Peak District

John Anthony

Shire Publications Ltd

CONTENTS

Set in 8 point Times and printed in Great Britain by C. I. Thomas & Sons (Haverfordwest) Ltd, Press Buildings, Merlins Bridge, Haverfordwest, Dyfed.

British Library Cataloguing in Publication data available.

ACKNOWLEDGEMENTS
   Photographs on the following pages are acknowledged to: the Automobile Association, 4; Derby City Council, 2, 31; Derby Museums and Art Gallery, 31, 32; Cadbury Lamb, cover, 7, 9, 18, 19, 35, 37, 41, 48, 49, 53; the Midland Railway Trust, 36; the Royal Crown Derby Porcelain Company Ltd, 33. All other photographs are by the author.

COVER: *The Derwent Valley from Millstone Edge near Hathersage.*

Assembly Rooms, Market Place, Derby.

The Edale valley from Mam Nick looking towards the plateau of Kinder Scout.

1
The Peak and the Lowlands

One of the delights of the English countryside is the diversity of the scenery and Derbyshire alone can show almost the entire range. This is due to its position on the border between highland and lowland Britain.

In the north-west of the county, the Peak District forms the southern end of the Pennine Chain of hills which extends like a backbone through northern England. To the south and east the country is much lower in height above sea level and entirely different in character for here one is immediately aware that one is in midland England. The differences are not merely ones of height. The uplands are generally sparsely peopled whereas the lowlands are an intensively settled landscape, even in some areas an urbanised landscape of industry and towns. Derbyshire, then, is a microcosm of Britain in that, except for the coast, one can see most types of British countryside in one county.

THE PEAK DISTRICT

Most of the northern part of the Peak District is formed of dark-coloured gritstone and this type of country extends southwards along the eastern and western flanks of the area. Between these flanks the greater part of the southern Peak District is formed of light-coloured limestone, which forms a rough plateau at about 1200 feet (365 m) above sea level. The gritstone, being more resistant to

weathering, forms higher land at about 2000 feet (610 m) and this is known as the High Peak. Because the dark gritstone gives a sombre colouring to the landscape, this area is also sometimes called the Dark Peak. Similarly the limestone country is known as the Low Peak or the White Peak.

The High Peak

To many people the high gritstone country is the real Peak District. This vast plateau is deeply eroded by fast-flowing streams and much of the area is covered by a thick mass of peat, bearing a distinctive vegetation of cotton grass with heather on the lower slopes. Although never more than 20 miles (30 km) from the heart of either Manchester or Sheffield, here a walker can tramp all day without seeing another human being and it is this possibility of solitude which is, perhaps, its greatest value today.

In contrast to the Low Peak with its network of minor roads and numerous villages, the High Peak is an austere world with only a few groups of houses here and there and no minor roads at all. Only the main routes form the road system and provide the key to this magnificent country. Further south, the gritstone moors flanking the limestone often form impressive cliff-like edges which dominate the valleys below. There are fine walks to be had along many of these edges, such as Baslow,

CHAPTER 1

Curbar and Froggatt Edges above the Derwent valley.

Between the limestone and the gritstone regions there are frequently areas of shale, which often produce lowland country on account of the friable nature of shale. Mam Tor above the Hope Valley is formed of shale and is often known as the shivering mountain as the shale is constantly disintegrating.

The Low Peak

This is the country of the Dales. Limestone is a rock readily dissolved by water and the streams have worn away these deep dales. The steep hillsides, almost always thickly wooded, rise on either side with the stream flowing rapidly over the rocks in the dale floor. Many of these streams have been dammed to form shallow pools for fish breeding and these pools and the little weirs alongside add much to the beauty of the scene.

Most of the dales are served by public footpaths and especially to be recommended are Lathkill Dale, Monsal Dale and the splendid succession of dales along the course of the river Dove: Beresford Dale, Mill Dale and the most famous of all, Dovedale.

The lowlands

The south of Derbyshire lies in the valley of the river Trent, often thought of as the 'frontier' between midland and northern England. Much of this is sandstone country, which has a distinctive reddish colour, most noticeable in freshly ploughed fields. Within the broad valley of the great river there is a generally flat, pastoral landscape but elsewhere the views are of gently rolling countryside with an occasional dramatic rocky outcrop of older rocks.

Along the eastern side of the county are the carboniferous rocks with the coal measures, and the mining of coal for many centuries has left indelible marks on this landscape. Interspersed with these mining areas there are stretches of country of a remarkably rural nature containing much of interest to the visitor. This combination of farm and coal mine is not without interest in itself. Many of the Derbyshire collieries have closed and great efforts are being made to deal with the abandoned colliery spoil heaps and buildings by clearing dereliction and reshaping the heaps to more natural contours and planting grass and trees.

The viewpoint plaque at Holme Moss.

One of the millstone boundary signs erected at some of the entrances to the national park.

2
The Peak District National Park

The Peak District was the first of the ten areas of especially beautiful country in England and Wales to be made a national park. This was in 1951 and a special authority, the Peak Park Joint Planning Board, was set up to care for the beauty of the area, to provide suitable recreational facilities and to act as the planning authority in place of the usual local authorities.

There are 542 square miles (1404 sq km) of countryside in the national park and about half this area is within Derbyshire. The remainder extends into Staffordshire, Cheshire, South and West Yorkshire and Greater Manchester.

Walking in the Peak

The Peak District is pre-eminently walkers' country, ideal both for those out for just a leisurely stroll through pleasant countryside and for those for whom the rough going and scrambling of moorland walking have an irresistible appeal. While the charms of the Peak can be enjoyed from a motorcar, those who are prepared to park the car and walk even a short distance can see far more.

For the strollers it is probably the southern part of the Peak which has most to offer. The dales can nearly all be seen from footpaths which offer straightforward walking. Across the limestone uplands there is fine walking along the network of footpaths and minor lanes still little used by motor traffic.

The gritstone moorlands to the east and west of the limestone are not very high and can be safely traversed by walkers of modest abilities.

The main gritstone moors of the north of the national park represent more of a challenge to the walker. Kinder Scout, Bleaklow, Holme Moss and Derwent Moors are among the finest walking country in Britain and although there will be some people about on summer weekends at other times one can usually have the moor to oneself.

Although of moderate height, and not within the commonly accepted sense of the word mountains, these moors must be treated with respect, especially by those inexperienced in hill walking. Ability to use a map and compass, essential equipment, is required, for even in sunny summer weather mist can descend rapidly and increase the problems of navigation across moors where tracks of any kind are few. Members of the National Park

Ranger Service patrol the moors to assist walkers to get the best from their walk and to help anyone in trouble. A rescue service is always in readiness to deal with casualties, who fortunately are few as most walkers take sensible precautions beforehand. Warm waterproof clothing is essential at all times of the year and strong boots and a supply of spare food are also needed.

The Pennine Way, the first of the long-distance footpaths created under the National Parks and Access to the Countryside Act, 1949, starts at Edale on its 250 mile (400 km) journey along the backbone of the Pennines to Kirk Yetholm on the Scottish border. Much of this walking is arduous and only for the experienced walker. Several guide books to the Pennine Way are available to assist those contemplating the walk but most visitors to the Peak will content themselves with walking just the southern end.

Access to the countryside

The fact that this area is a national park does not mean that the whole area is public property. The great majority of the land continues to be in private ownership and public access can only be by public roads and footpaths in the usual way. Even so there are a number of ways in which special provision has been made to enable people to enjoy the country. Foremost among these are the access agreements between the National Park Board and certain landowners which allow one to go anywhere over some 76 square miles (197 sq km) of moorland, subject only to some commonsense byelaws and, in some cases, to closure on a few days in late summer for grouse shooting. Some agreements allow the owner to close his moor for a maximum of twelve days in the shooting season (12th August to 10th December). Any normal public right of way is not affected. A list of closure dates is prepared on a monthly basis and is obtainable from the National Park Office or information centres. Signs are displayed at entry points around the closed areas on the days concerned.

There is a long story of effort, since the nineteenth century, to obtain the freedom of these hills for the people. Thousands in the nearby industrial cities such as Sheffield and Manchester could see the vast, empty and beautiful moorlands yet could not legally set foot upon them. Pressure grew, especially in the 1930s, and on Sunday 24th April 1932 there was an organised mass trespass on Kinder Scout by some of the more militant members of the movement. Six men were arrested and subsequently sentenced to prison terms of between two and six months. There were further mass trespasses but the more traditional members of the access movement stood aside from such action, and even in some

cases condemned it, and very slowly a little progress was made until the National Parks and Access to the Countryside Act, 1949, provided for access agreements with landowners, or in default of agreement for access orders.

With such a vexed history, the official inauguration of the first of these access agreements, on Kinder Scout, held in the little square outside the Nag's Head Inn, Edale, on Good Friday of 1954 was a significant event, not only in the history of access to the Peak District, but of access to the British countryside in general. The fiftieth anniversary of the 1932 Kinder Scout trespass was commemorated in some style in 1982 and a plaque now marks the quarry at Hayfield from which the trespassers set out. It is a story which is not yet concluded for there are many more moorlands, even in the Peak District, to which the public ought to have access.

Sports and pastimes

Apart from walking there are many other sporting activities available in the national park. Rock climbing is practised on the gritstone edges, where the climbs are tricky enough for the most experienced exponent of the craft, although not of any great length. Nevertheless the Peak climbs have been the training ground of many a climber who subsequently distinguished himself in the Alps or even the Himalayas.

Skiing is sometimes possible for short periods, the most favoured places being near Buxton, close to the Chapel-en-le-Frith to Castleton road and at Edale, where the National Park Board owns some suitable land. On the few days when the sport is possible vast numbers of hopeful skiiers throng the roads in these areas.

In the limestone country the solubility of the rock has resulted in many caves and underground passages, which are explored by enthusiastic potholers. Although of great fascination to its devotees, the sport is dangerous and should on no account be attempted except under the guidance of one of the several clubs in the district. The Castleton and Matlock areas are the main centres of this activity. In both these places a number of caverns have been arranged with steps, paths and electric lighting and are open to the public for a small charge (see chapter 10).

At Great Hucklow the Lancashire and Derbyshire Gliding Club makes use of the currents of rising air caused by Hucklow Edge and a glider may often be seen soaring noiselessly in the air above the countryside.

Fishing is an important activity in the streams of the Peak, especially in the limestone country. Almost all the waters are strictly preserved but some of the hotels own fishing

Ladybower reservoir.

rights which are available to their guests. Fishing is also possible in some of the reservoirs, notably the Ladybower and Derwent Reservoirs.

A hilly area such as the Peak District is hardly ideal cycling country but throughout the rest of Derbyshire conditions are excellent. Even in the Peak the number of cyclists is increasing and in some places cycles are provided for hire to visitors who arrive by car or public transport. The cycle hire centres are mainly related to the trail routes described in chapter 3 and are to be found at Middleton Top, Parsley Hay and Ashbourne on the High Peak and Tissington Trail; at Waterhouses at the southern end of the Manifold Valley track; at Hayfield at the eastern end of the Sett Valley Trail; at Fairholmes in the Upper Derwent Valley and at Lyme Park. Full details of these facilities are obtainable from the National Park Office, Baslow Road, Bakewell DE4 1AE; telephone Bakewell (0629) 814321, extension 214.

There are private cycle hire centres at Hartington, telephone Hartington (029 884) 459; Hope, telephone Hope Valley (0433) 20535; Monsal Head, telephone Great Longstone (062 987) 505; Tissington, telephone Parwich (033 525) 455; Thorpe, telephone Thorpe Cloud (033 529) 410; and at Waterhouses, telephone Waterhouses (053 86) 313.

Undoubtedly the most popular form of recreation is that of simply driving, or being driven, in a motor vehicle to see the scenery of the national park. For this the Peak is equipped with excellent roads, few of which are as narrow and tortuous as those which have to be negotiated in so many areas of hill country. Parking can be a problem in some very popular places, and all over the national park on fine summer weekends.

Information about the national park

Current information about the national park is contained in *The Peakland Post*, which is published each spring and can be obtained from the National Park Office, Baslow Road, Bakewell DE4 1AE free of charge on receipt of a stamp. In the park there is a ranger service provided by full-time rangers with seasonal part-time and voluntary assistance. The rangers will often be seen about the park, frequently with their distinctive vehicles, and they are there to help the visitor. On moorland access land they are especially important in helping walkers.

There are three information centres open throughout the year: Bakewell, Old Market Hall, in the town centre, telephone Bakewell (0629) 813227; Edale, Fieldhead, on the road between the station and the village, telephone Hope Valley (0433) 70207; Castleton, Castle Street, telephone Hope Valley (0433) 20679. During the winter the information centre at Castleton closes mid-week and that at Bakewell on Thursday.

In addition to these centres there is a mobile information centre in a caravan and small information points at Fairholmes near Derwent Dam, at the old signal box at Hartington on the Tissington Trail, and at Derbyshire Bridge in the Goyt Valley.

For those in need of more extensive information and who wish to engage in systematic study of the national park there is the National Park Study Centre at Losehill Hall, Castleton. This was formerly a guest house and now accommodates up to sixty people, usually for a few days, but organised groups can make day visits and there are facilities for organisations to arrange their own functions there. Full details of the range of residential courses, seminars and activity holidays can be obtained for a stamped addressed envelope sent to: The Principal, Losehill Hall, Castleton, Sheffield S30 2WB; telephone Hope Valley (0433) 20373.

Public transport

Rail services are limited in the Peak District. The *Derbyshire Wayfarer* scheme provides for a single ticket at a standard price entitling the holder to travel for one day almost anywhere in the county, and to certain places beyond, by bus and on most rail routes. Details are obtainable from the Public Transport Unit, Derbyshire County Council, FREEPOST, Matlock DE4 9BR. A similar scheme, the *Wayfarer* ticket, is operated by Greater Manchester Transport providing for travel within Greater Manchester and the National Park. Details are obtainable from Greater Manchester Transport, PO Box 429, 9 Portland Street, Manchester M60 1HX.

Derbyshire County Council produces a *Peak District Public Transport Timetable* obtainable, price 40p, at information centres throughout the area or by post from the Public Transport Unit, Freepost, Matlock DE4 9BR.

Where to stay

There is a great range of hotels, guest houses, youth hostels, boarding houses and householders offering bed and breakfast accommodation throughout the area but especially in the Peak District. A guide to accommodation in the national park and a booking service to callers at the Bakewell information centre are provided by the National Park Board. They also provide 'camping barns'. These are traditional stone barns that have outlived their agricultural usefulness and now serve as 'stone tents'. Users need normal camping equipment except for the tent. Details are obtainable from the National Park Office, Baslow Road, Bakewell DE4 1AE.

Buildings of the Peak

Visitors new to the Peak District are impressed by the fact that all the buildings are of stone and even the fields are separated by stone walls instead of hedges. In former times it was impossible to transport building materials as cheaply and easily as today and so local materials, whatever was to hand on the spot,

had to be used.

In the Peak this meant stone and the use of a single material gives a remarkable homogeneity to the district. One immediately knows when one passes out of the Peak District for brick buildings appear and strike the eye as being strange if one has been in the Peak long enough to get used to the stone.

Within the district gritstone and limestone are used each in their own areas. In the far north, near Saddleworth and Holmfirth, the gritstone can be quarried in long thin slabs, which skilled craftsmen built into long low houses with many small windows with heavy mullions. Further south the gritstone is more intractable and imposes austerity upon the massive buildings capped by flattish pitched roofs of heavy stone slabs.

The limestone is more responsive to the mason's chisel but was still used in a massive way to build the characteristic buildings of the Low Peak. Where the two districts join both kinds of stone are to be found in the same village, and even in the same building, as at Bakewell, Hartington and Castleton.

An invaluable aid in keeping many traditional buildings in the district is the Derbyshire Historic Buildings Trust. This is a voluntary organisation which operates a 'revolving fund', which is used to buy old buildings in need of repair, restore them, frequently introducing such modern amenities as plumbing, and then put them up for sale so that the money may be used to purchase more buildings in danger. The trust has been especially successful in repairing modest buildings such as cottages, which, whilst not important enough to attract widespread attention, are yet important in their setting and whose demolition would leave an unpleasant gap.

Today the cost of building in stone is appreciably greater than that of using brick or other materials. Yet the distinctive appearance of the Peak depends upon the continued use of stone whilst the inhabitants must be allowed to erect new buildings. The solution of the problem has been found in the use of reconstituted stone blocks, which make use of small pieces of stone pressed into the surface of a block of concrete. These blocks greatly reduce costs although fortunately some new buildings are still built of stone in the traditional manner.

Using these traditional materials is important if the essential character of the Peak is to be maintained, for the buildings are often an important element in the landscape. But this does not mean that new buildings must follow the old in all the details of their design. There is ample scope for new ideas and the visitor will see buildings of purely twentieth-century design which respect the local traditions in materials and thus in colour and texture.

Heavy stone slabs, graded in size, roof this building on the boundary of Hathersage churchyard.

Reservoirs

One of the most valuable products of the Peak District today is pure water supplied to nearby towns, and indeed to much further afield. Many valleys in the district are suitable for damming to provide reservoirs in which to collect the water which flows off the moorland. Since the 1830s many such reservoirs have been built. The gathering grounds for these reservoirs occupy nearly one third of the area of the national park and this includes most of the northern part of the park.

Especially noticeable are the reservoirs which stretch along 5 miles (8 km) of Longdendale and the three great reservoirs which supply water to Sheffield, Derby, Nottingham and Leicester. These are in the upper valley of the river Derwent. For the lowest of the three, Ladybower Reservoir, two villages were cleared before the valley was flooded in the 1940s. During exceptionally dry summers the level of the water falls so low that the foundations of the buildings of Derwent village can be seen and one can walk down what was once the village street.

To the south-west of Wirksworth, between the villages of Hopton and Hognaston, the new Carsington Reservoir is being built. Covering some 725 acres (293 ha), the reservoir will provide facilities for boating, fishing, boardsailing and sub-aqua swimming. Around the lake will be new footpaths, a horse-riding trail and several car parks. There is to be a main reception centre for visitors a little to the north of Hognaston village off the B5035 road.

Farming

The visitor to the Peak District is usually interested in the fine country around him. Although this may at first seem to be the work of nature, the farmer has also taken a hand in evolving the pattern of the countryside.

Farming in the Peak is mostly livestock rearing for, except on the better lands of the valley floors, the depth and fertility of the soil make it unsuitable for cultivation. On the higher lands which make up the greater part of the national park the farmsteads are found typically in sheltered positions in the valleys or part way up the hillsides. The farm buildings of grey stone are often sheltered by a group of sycamores and one can still find many examples of house and farm buildings combined in a single long, low structure under a roof of heavy stone slates. They seem to be embattled against the rigours of the climate.

Sheep are the predominant form of livestock to be seen in the district, the Derbyshire Gritstone sheep being a characteristic sight on the moors, although many other breeds are to be seen on the lower lands. Dairying is the mainstay of farming in the limestone country, with the milk being supplied direct to nearby towns and to processing works, which have been set up in several places in the Peak. Cheese making was once an important local activity but is now restricted to a single factory at Hartington.

Elvaston Castle, viewed from its elaborate gardens.

3
The Derbyshire countryside

Whilst the visitor to Derbyshire will always be drawn to the splendours of the Peak District, other parts of the county have much to offer and would amply justify its fame quite apart from the Peak District.

COUNTRY PARKS

Buxton Country Park, Green Lane, Buxton. Telephone: Buxton (0298) 6978. *Buxton Civic Association.*

Grin Low Woods comprise almost 100 acres (40 ha) of woodland planted in 1820 to hide scars caused by quarrying. The woods now have a rich ground flora and there are fine walks through the woods leading to Solomon's Temple, a folly 25 feet (7.6 m) high and built in 1895. It stands on a tumulus of the neolithic period. There is a spiral staircase inside and from the top are wide views over the surrounding country. To the south at Grinlow are a car park and picnic area.

The most remarkable feature of this country park is Poole's Cavern. There is an admission charge for this cave, although the woods are always open free of charge. Formed by the waters of the river Wye, the cave has impressive stalactites and stalagmites and these can be seen in comfort as there are only sixteen steps to be negotiated and the whole cavern is illuminated by electricity. At the cavern entrance is an audio-visual display about the cave.

Elvaston Castle Country Park and Elvaston Working Estate Museum, Elvaston, Derby DE7 3EP. Telephone: Derby (0332) 71342. 5 miles (8 km) south-east of Derby. *Derbyshire County Council.*

The 200 acres (80 ha) of the gardens and park of Elvaston Castle, formerly the residence of the Earls of Harrington, became a country park in 1970. The gardens were laid out in the 1830s and 1840s by William Barron for the fourth Earl and the evergreen planting is especially notable. Much restoration work has been carried out in the gardens, and the parterre before the south front of the castle was planted in 1970 to replace features that had decayed beyond repair.

Extensive car parks have been laid out, all planted in a way of which Barron would surely have approved, and there are camping sites for tents and touring caravans. There is a riding school, tea rooms, shop and displays on the history of the place.

The Working Estate Museum shows how such a great estate functioned at the beginning of the twentieth century, with a close-knit community of labourers and craftsmen, tradesmen and their families. Some of the outbuildings have been restored to show their work and old breeds of livestock and old farm machinery are on display. Museum staff in period costume help to recreate the period and demonstrations of working methods take place. An information centre and nature trail complete the facilities.

Hardwick Hall Country Park, Doe Lea, Chesterfield S44 5QJ. Telephone: Chesterfield (0246) 850430. 5 miles (8 km) north-west of Mansfield, alongside the M1 motorway, from which it is accessible at junction 29 by following signs. *National Trust.*

The great house of Bess of Hardwick dominates the ridge and below, on the westward-facing slope, 250 acres (100 ha) of the park have been set aside as a country park, always open but separately from the hall and gardens. There is a visitor centre and a nature trail, which passes by the Hardwick Oak, said to be four hundred years old. Coarse fishing is available by permit in several fishponds and the old Hardwick Inn is nearby for refreshment. Hardwick park is valuable in allowing the visitor to see an old park as many such hunting parks must have appeared long before the vogue for landscaping them into elegant settings for country houses. At Hardwick the park was left unaltered for several centuries and the flock of Whiteface Woodland sheep and the herd of Longhorn cattle add to the impression of rugged, ancient parkland.

Ilam Country Park, Ilam, Ashbourne. Telephone: Thorpe Cloud (033 529) 245. *National Trust.*

The estate at Ilam was presented to the National Trust in 1934, although much extended since then. 84 acres (34 ha) of the woods and parkland are now a country park, open to the public free of charge at all times. The village is an estate village built in the 1840s and 1850s with much tile-hanging, steep gables and fancy bargeboards. The hall was built by the Watts-Russell family in 1821-6 to designs by John Shaw the elder but only part now remains, adapted as a youth hostel. There

is a National Trust information centre and shop and a tea shop. A booklet of walks is available which enables one to appreciate the great beauty and interest of this park. The river Manifold flows underground from Wetton Mill to reappear at boil holes within the park. Only at times of exceptional rainfall does the river flow along the surface. Traces remain of the gardens of the hall and of the ridge and furrow of the open fields of the medieval village.

Longshaw, Foxhouse, Sheffield S11 7TZ. 7 miles (11 km) south-west of Sheffield, bounded by A625, B6055 and B6054. *National Trust.*

Here are more than 1000 acres (400 ha) of open moorlands and woodlands which, together with farmland, make up the Longshaw Estate, purchased mainly by public subscription in the 1930s. Longshaw Lodge was a shooting lodge of the Dukes of Rutland and was built about 1827 but it is now converted into flats. Close by are an information centre, shop and cafe. There is a nature trail and facilities for horse riding but the outstanding activities at Longshaw have long been walking and climbing, for which this rocky gritstone moorland is admirably suited.

Longshaw has always been especially loved by the people of Sheffield and the Sheffield buses run to the Fox House Inn by the junction of A625 and B6055. The inn is of the seventeenth century and has been much restored so that appreciation of its Brontë associations requires some effort of the imagination.

Lyme Park, Disley, Stockport, Cheshire SK12 2NX. Telephone: Disley (066 32) 2023. To the south of Disley; the entrance is just west of the village on the A6 road to Stockport. *National*

Hardwick Hall seen above one of the elaborately crested garden walls.

Trust, managed by Stockport Metropolitan Borough Council.

Lyme was owned by the Legh family for exactly six hundred years until 1946 and the park is an ancient one formed from part of Macclesfield Forest. Red deer roam the park, which extends up the surrounding hills to the high moors around.

This is a park of fine walking country. There are pools and several buildings dotted about the park, such as Lyme Cage, a tower originally built in the 1520s, although later altered, to serve as a viewpoint from which to watch hunting in the park.

Shipley Country Park, Slack Lane, Heanor Gate, Heanor DE7 7GX. Telephone: Langley Mill (0773) 719961 or 715480. Between Heanor and Ilkeston. Main entrance signposted from A608 in Heanor. Further entrances from A6007 and A609 through Mapperley village. *Derbyshire County Council.*

Shipley Country Park is an outstanding example of turning a liability into an asset. The main area of the park was once the Shipley Hall estate of the Miller-Munday family. They left in 1922 and the hall and grounds were neglected until the house was demolished in 1943 because of mining subsidence. There is a long history of coal mining in the area and this, combined with other industrial exploitation, resulted in a devastated landscape. In 1970 the opencast working of coal began over 500 acres (200 ha) and some 1.5 million tons of coal have been extracted. The restoration works have been carried out in close collaboration with the county council to produce a new landscape, which, although incorporating some features of the old one, is designed to serve as a regional leisure centre. The work has involved clearing derelict colliery buildings and stopping up thirty mine shafts. Shipley Lake has had to be re-made. The entire project will take many years, and coal working is still in progress on adjoining areas, but already there is a park of 815 acres (330 ha) out of a total area of some 1000 acres (400 ha). This occupies the western part of the area; the eastern side is occupied by the American Adventure theme park (see chapter 9).

Facilities already available include a visitor centre, footpaths, bridleways, cycle routes, picnic places and fishing, the last available by permit. The western area remains to be developed but there is a riding centre at Lodge Farm and on Shipley Lake there is sailing. A golf course is proposed for the future.

The site of Shipley Hall is now a picnic site and many of the fine trees survive, although no other traces remain of the once elaborate gardens. Some buildings have survived, including one called 'The Garden' of 1882 which was possibly the dower house of the hall, the Home Farm, which was designed by William Eden Nesfield in 1861, and the Derby and Nottingham Lodges of 1911, designed by Sir Edwin Lutyens.

On the southern edge of the park is Mapperley Reservoir, constructed in 1821 as a feeder reservoir for the Nutbrook Canal. Here there are pleasant walks by the water, fishing by permit and a nature trail. To the east of the dam is a nature reserve which is not open to the public.

TRAILS AND TRACKS

Several of the numerous tracks of closed railways have been converted into routes for walkers, cyclists and horse riders.

Five Pits Trail

This 7½ mile (11.7 km) trail between Tibshelf and Temple Normanton has been developed from the sites of five large collieries and the connecting railway tracks. Since the closure of the last of the collieries in 1973 some of the land has been reclaimed for industry, agriculture and forestry and the trail has been created for use by walkers, cyclists and horse riders. The trail lies close to the M1 motorway to the south-east of Chesterfield and has four car parks. There is a ranger service operating from 23 Market Street, Clay Cross, telephone: Chesterfield (0246) 866960.

High Peak and Tissington Trails.

The High Peak Trail and the Tissington Trail together form the most extensive of these trails. The former is 17½ miles (28 km) long and the latter adds 10½ miles (17 km) to form a Y-shaped network.

The High Peak Trail had its origin in the Cromford and High Peak Railway, which was one of the earliest railways in Britain. Indeed it was so early, being opened in 1830, that it was not built to form part of the railway system but as a link in the canal system, joining the Peak Forest Canal at Whaley Bridge to the Cromford Canal at Cromford. The rugged nature of the country between ruled out a canal connection and Josiah Jessop built this railway 33 miles (53 km) long. Wagons were hauled by horses on the level sections and on the steep inclines stationary steam engines operated a system whereby six empty wagons acted as a counterweight to three loaded wagons. The horses were replaced by steam locomotives in the mid nineteenth century and the line was closed in 1967.

The track was purchased jointly by the Peak Park Planning Board and the county council and added to the Tissington Trail, which had been bought by the board a little earlier. This had formed part of the Ashbourne to Buxton line and the trail extends from north of the junction with the High Peak Trail at Parsley Hay to Mapleton, north Ashbourne.

Middleton Top Engine House, where the original Butterley beam engine is preserved. Built in 1829 it hauled wagons up the incline on the Cromford and High Peak Railway.

A number of the old railway buildings have been retained and adapted to new uses. The signal box at Hartington is now an information point, the Wharf Shed at Cromford and Hopton Cottage are now self-catering hostels and the railway workshops at High Peak Junction have been restored with an exhibition on the railway, a model, shop and information centre; telephone Wirksworth (062 982) 2831. The engine house and engine at the top of the Middleton Incline (see chapter 9) have both been restored, the engine having been made by the Butterley Company in 1829. There is an information centre and cycles may be hired; telephone Wirksworth (062 982) 3204.

Manifold Track

In 1904 a curious railway was opened along the Manifold Valley between Hulme End and Waterhouses. The gauge was 30 inches (762 mm) and it was modelled on a light railway in India. The railway closed in 1934 and the track was converted into a tarmac footpath. Some of the station buildings remain at Hulme End and there is a short, unlit tunnel at Swainsley. The section between Swainsley and Wettonmill is a road also used by motor vehicles.

Monsal Trail

This trail has been created from the track of the old Midland Railway main line which once ran from London (St Pancras) to Manchester. The line was closed in 1968 and twelve years later the National Park Board took over the track. There are four long tunnels which have had to be closed and links have been made around these using ordinary footpaths or special concession paths so that one can walk the entire 7 miles (11 km). Between Little Longstone and Monsal Head a short length of minor road has to be used. There are car park, toilets and a Ranger Centre at Miller's Dale station and car parks at Monsal Head and Bakewell station. Some parts are very steep and care must be taken to keep to the path. Only the section from Bakewell to Longstone is at present surfaced so that cyclists, horse riders and wheelchair users may follow this section. The remainder, to just beyond Miller's Dale, has only the rough railway ballast surface so that stout footwear is required.

Sett Valley Trail

The railway linking New Mills and Hayfield was opened in 1868 and closed in 1970. The county council purchased the track in 1973 and provided car parking at either end of the 2½ mile (4 km) route and a picnic site at Hayfield, where cycles may be hired; telephone New Mills (0663) 46222. The trail is joined by the Torrs industrial heritage trail and many other footpaths connect. There are good views of the country, with the large mill buildings mainly used for calico printing and paper making and using the fast-flowing water of the river Sett on its way down from Kinder Scout.

PICNIC SITES

There are several small areas of countryside which offer opportunities for parking the car, having a picnic and enjoying fine views of the countryside.

Outstanding among these is **White Lodge,** off the A6 road some 2 miles (3 km) west of Ashford-in-the-Water. From here one can walk into the incomparable Monsal Dale.

At **Black Rocks,** off the B5036 road, 1 mile (1.6 km) south of Cromford, the wooded remains of old quarries have been adapted as a picnic site and the rocks are a valuable training ground for climbers.

Highoredish, 3 miles (5 km) east of Matlock off the B6014 road, provides 16 acres (6.5 ha) of spectacular hillside with views over the Ogston Reservoir. An Automobile Association viewfinder helps to identify places of interest that can be seen.

At **Tideswell Dale,** off the B6049 road, a mile (1.6 km) south of Tideswell, an attractive picnic area has been created from a site cleared of derelict quarry plant.

GOYT VALLEY

The valley of the headwaters of the river Goyt, to the north-west of Buxton, is now dominated by the Fernilee and Errwood Reservoirs, which were constructed in 1938 and 1968 respectively. Once the valley had a thriving agricultural community alongside Errwood Hall and there were also a paint mill and a gunpowder factory. All this has now gone and today there are only great woodlands around the two reservoirs. The beauty of the valley, although very different from that of the past, is nevertheless still there and vast numbers of people visit the Goyt valley today, although there is virtually no resident population.

These special circumstances suggested an experiment in managing the impact of visitors on a landscape. In 1970 there began a ban on motor traffic along the valley road between The Street and Derbyshire Bridge, just north of A537, on summer weekends. Visitors leave their cars at special free car parks and can then enjoy the pleasures of the valley without interference from the internal combustion engine. Adjoining the car parks are waymarked walks, a nature trail and picnic places. There is an information point at Derbyshire Bridge.

At all other times, whether the traffic management scheme is in operation or not, traffic is one way from The Street to Derbyshire Bridge.

UPPER DERWENT VALLEY

The three great reservoirs, Howden, Derwent and Ladybower, which occupy the upper valley of the river Derwent, have the effect of making the road along the west side of the reservoirs a cul-de-sac north of the A57 Glossop to Sheffield road, and a traffic management scheme operates on summer Sundays and bank holidays. The road beyond Fairholmes, just below the Derwent Dam, is closed to all motor vehicles save those of disabled people and a minibus service, which operates as far as King's Tree near the northern end of Howden Reservoir.

The car park at Fairholmes is available at all times and here there is an information point, toilets and a cycle hire centre. There are waymarked footpaths, cycle routes and bridleways. Trout fishing is available on Derwent and Ladybower reservoirs, with boats for hire by fishermen. Permits for fishing are obtainable from the Fishery Warden's office on the road to Bamford, A6013.

4
Customs and events

In former times Derbyshire was a remote county and many old customs and traditions, not to say superstitions, have survived here longer than elsewhere.

Well dressing

Foremost of these ancient customs is well dressing, the decoration of wells or springs with boards bearing pictures made from flower petals or other natural materials. The custom is undoubtedly a very ancient one, possibly going back to the pre-Christian period, then adopted by Christianity and adapted to its purposes. Possibly the custom grew up from attempts to placate the water gods, and then to give thanks for the gift of a supply of pure water.

Today religious overtones are still strong in well dressing, providing the majority of the subjects for the pictures, and a service, usually interdenominational, is normally held to bless the wells. Where several wells are dressed in one village, the clergy and villagers usually walk in procession to each well.

The methods used to prepare the decorations vary from place to place, but all depend on a supply of suitable clay. This is found locally where possible. The clay is puddled with water and salt to the right consistency and is then applied to boards, framed with timber. These boards have numerous nails knocked into them to provide a key to hold the clay when applied to a thickness of about half an inch (13 mm). All the timber supports have to be well soaked previously as it is important that the clay retains its moisture for as long as possible. The salt is included to limit cracking as well as to help conserve moisture.

The design is prepared on paper, which is then placed over the surface of the clay and pricked through with an awl or some other sharp tool. Usually this outline in pin pricks is then emphasised by pressing in berries of holly or rowan or alder cones.

The main work of filling in the spaces and making the picture then begins with pressing in the longer lasting materials such as mosses, lichens and pieces of bark. The flowers follow; in some places just the petals, in other places whole flowers are used. The workers start at the bottom, each petal overlapping the one below like slates on a roof, so that rain will run down the picture without spoiling the effect. The hard work involved is prodigious but always felt to be well worthwhile.

Far from being an old custom in danger of dying out, well dressing is expanding and many more villages now dress their wells than was the case even in the 1960s. One of the main incentives is raising money for charity, as a collection box is always left beside the well. Frequently the village carnival will take place at the same time as the well dressing.

Well dressing takes place at the following places. The dates given are in some cases approximate and are the dates of the first dressing of the well. The wells are usually worth visting for up to a week after the dressing, depending on the weather. The list is not necessarily complete and no responsibility can be taken for its accuracy. Up-to-date information can be obtained from tourist information centres in all the towns.

Ashford-in-the Water, Saturday before Trinity Sunday.
Bakewell, last Saturday in June.
Barlow, Wednesday after St Lawrence's Day (10th August).
Bonsall, usually the last Saturday in July.
Bradwell, usually the first Monday in August.
Buxton, usually during the second week in July.
Cutthorpe, July.
Derby, Chester Green, Saturday before Late Spring Bank Holiday.
Edlaston, last Sunday in June.
Etwall, May.
Eyam, last Saturday in August.
Heath, Ault Hucknall and Holmewood, one well at each village, mid July.
Hope, last Saturday in June.
Litton, Saturday nearest St John the Baptist's Day (24th June).
Monyash, first week in June.
Pilsley, mid July.
Stoney Middleton, usually the last Saturday in July.

Tideswell, Saturday nearest St John the Baptist's Day (24th June).
Tissington, Ascension Day.
West Hallam, mid summer.
Whitwell, usually the third Saturday in July.
Wirksworth, Saturday before Late Spring Bank Holiday.
Wormhill, Saturday before Late Spring Bank Holiday.
Youlgreave, Saturday nearest St John the Baptist's Day (24th June).

Church customs
A number of old customs are connected with churches. The most obviously so is perhaps that of church 'clypping' or 'clipping'. The congregation files out of church and forms a ring round the building, holding hands. A hymn is sung and the ceremony ends with a blessing. The custom is observed at Wirksworth and at Burbage near Buxton and the name may be derived from the old verb to 'clip', meaning to embrace. Hence the custom may be a ceremonial act of embracing the church. The real origin is unknown.

In some churches garlands of paper flowers may be seen, occasionally framing a pair of white paper gloves. These are the symbols of purity carried at the funerals of unmarried girls and left hanging in the church afterwards.

Well dressing at Bradwell.

SAMUEL ANOINTS DAVID

BRADWELL

CHAPTER 4

Garland Day, Castleton

At Castleton the well known Garland Day celebration takes place on Oakapple Day, 29th May, anniversary of the restoration of Charles II in 1660. The garland is a massive construction of wood covered with straw, to which are tied bunches of leaves and wild flowers. This is carried round the village mounted on a 'King' and accompanied by a 'Queen' dressed in Stuart costume, with a silver band. Finally the garland is hoisted off the shoulders of the 'King' up to one of the pinnacles of the church tower, to remain there until the end of the week. Whilst the custom certainly dates back to the seventeenth century, some believe it to be much older and to be connected with pagan fertility rites of the coming of summer.

Plague Sunday, Eyam

This commemoration dates back only to 1905 but serves to remind us of the terrors of pestilence to our forefathers. The plague was carried to this remote village at the time of the Great Plague of London in 1665 and 259 inhabitants died within a year out of the seventy six families in the village.

On the last Sunday in August a procession starts from the church and proceeds to Cucklett Dell or Cucklett Church, a field where the Reverend William Mompesson, the rector, held services during the plague in the hope of lessening the risk of infection. His devoted service to his flock is always commemorated, as is that of the Reverend Thomas Stanley, the previous rector, who had been ejected a few years before as a puritan but who still lived in the village and unselfishly helped Mompesson to cope with the dreadful times. For this reason it is appropriate that the service is always interdenominational.

Other customs

Several villages still ring the curfew, a practice ordered by William the Conqueror and surviving still in other parts of England. At Winster the 'Gallups' or Pancake Race is still carried on, and at Padley there is the Pilgrimage, a procession in commemoration of Roman Catholic priests executed at Derby in 1588. Ashbourne is famous for its Shrovetide football.

Agricultural shows

Bakewell Show, held in early August, formerly had the distinction of being the biggest one-day show in Britain. Although the show is no smaller, the claim cannot now be sustained as the events now take place over two days. There are all manner of attractions for the visiting townsman who wishes to see the country come to town but the splendour of the setting in the meadows of the Wye is justification enough for a day at Bakewell Show.

The Derbyshire County Show has a home at Elvaston Castle. Smaller agricultural shows are held at Ashbourne, Ashover, Hope and Moor Green and the Ashby-de-la-Zouch Show is held at Calke Abbey.

The horse trials each September at Chatsworth Park now have a national reputation. There are sheepdog trials at some agricultural shows but they are held on their own at Longshaw, Lyme and Dovedale (at Ilam).

Information

A complete list of events in the national park, giving details of dates and times, is included in *The Peakland Post*, issued each spring by the National Park Board (see chapter 2).

Creswell Crags, seen from the south of the artificial lake which now occupies the floor of the limestone gorge. The caves, in which the earliest remains of man in Britain have been found, are on either side of the gorge.

Arbor Low, the late neolithic henge monument near Monyash.

5
Ancient sites

Derbyshire and the Peak are rich in the remains of the past activities of man and the following account is but an outline mentioning some of the most important places.

PALAEOLITHIC
Creswell Crags, Cresswell (map reference SK 535742).

2 miles (3 km) east of Clowne, just off the A616, is a short gorge cut by a river. Into the sides of the gorge twenty-four caves and rock shelters have been found, containing remains of early man dating back to the time of the last interglacial period. This was about seventy thousand years ago, when man appears to have been sharing his environment with large mammals such as hippopotamus, hyena, bears and woolly rhinoceros. Creswell Crags are therefore of the greatest importance to the study of early man in Britain and frequent excavations have taken place. This work is still in progress.

The site is accessible to the public, although entry to the caves themselves is not possible. There is a visitor centre with an exhibition and an audio-visual programme which explains the significance of the place. These facilities are operated jointly by Derbyshire and Nottinghamshire County Councils as the county boundary runs through the gorge.

Creswell Crags have another interest in that George Stubbs (1724-1806), best known as the outstanding animal painter of his time, used

this place as the setting for many of his paintings. During the 1760s he painted many pictures of horses in a state of nature, of horses attacked by a lion and of other animals such as leopards near the mouths of the caves. This was a very remote place at that time, long before the road was made through the gorge and long before the discovery of remains of prehistoric man and animals, first reported in 1874.

Other palaeolithic sites
There have been many other discoveries of the remains of the activities of early man and animals in Derbyshire. In the early nineteenth century the skeleton of a woolly rhinoceros was found in Dream Cave near Wirksworth and in 1903 bones of a sabre-toothed tiger and an early form of horse were found at Dove Holes near Buxton. Valuable discoveries have been made in caves in the Manifold Valley and near Earl Sterndale.

NEOLITHIC
Neolithic man has left traces of his existence in the shape of chambered barrows at **Mininglow** (SK 209572) and at **Five Wells** near Taddington (SK 124711). These are circular barrows with massive but ruined rock chambers for burials and they are probably the last remaining such structures, owing their survival to their remote locations.

Neolithic man is also represented by re-

17

CHAPTER 5

The Nine Ladies on Stanton Moor.

mains of his stone circles, which exist in a number of places in the area. Outstanding among them is Arbor Low.

Arbor Low, Middleton (map reference SK 160636).

3 miles (5 km) west of Youlgreave and close to the Parsley Hay to Youlgreave road, this is much the most spectacular prehistoric site in Derbyshire. The site, on the lonely limestone plateau, contributes much to the impressiveness of this important circular henge monument. There is a bank about 7 feet (2.1 m) high and 250 feet (76 m) in diameter, within which is a ditch from which the bank was excavated. There are entrances to the enclosure to the north and south and within the banked area is a circle of some fifty stones. These may once have been standing, but now all lie flat. At the centre is a U-shaped assembly of stones, close to which a skeleton was found. Arbor Low belongs to the late neolithic and early bronze age, about 2000 to 1600 BC.

Associated with Arbor Low are round barrows of somewhat later date. The principal one is that known as **Gib Hill,** about 350 yards (320 m) to the south-west.

Comparisons with Stonehenge are inevitable but Arbor Low, although less impressive, is enhanced by the remoteness of its setting and the visitor will be unfortunate if his experience is marred by crowds of other visitors. The site is accessible to the public under the guardianship of English Heritage.

There is another, less impressive henge monument at Dove Holes, known as the **Bull Ring,** (SK 078783), but all the stones are now gone.

BRONZE AGE

The **Nine Ladies** on Stanton Moor (SK 250635) is a circle of nine stones 33 feet (10 m) in diameter and is the best known of a complex assemblage of about seventy stone and ring cairns. The area on the gritstone plateau above the Derwent Valley to the west of Darley Dale appears to have been used as a place of worship and as a cemetery in the early bronze age (2000 to 1400 BC). Other remains of the period include the circle of **Nine Stones** on Harthill Moor (SK 225626) and there are more traces of stone circles on Froggatt Edge, (SK 249768) and Beeley Moor (SK 282685).

Round barrows are scattered about much of the Peak, usually datable to the bronze age, and many were first investigated by Thomas Bateman of Middleton-by-Youlgreave in the middle of the nineteenth century.

IRON AGE

There are earthworks belonging to the class known as hillforts at **Fin Cop** (SK 174710) above Monsal Dale, on **Coombs Moss** (SK 053783) and on **Mam Tor** (SK 128837). **Carl Wark** (SK 259815) to the east of Hathersage is a rock fortress with walls nearly 10 feet (3 m) high. Although Mam Tor was begun in the bronze age, the main lifespan of these forts would have been in the last few centuries before the Roman Conquest.

ROMAN PERIOD

The importance of this area to the Romans was mainly as a source of lead. The area was on the edge of the fully romanised region to the south and east and for long periods conditions may have been unsettled. Occupation of the Peak District, where the lead mines were situated, is likely to have been mainly by forts, of which the one usually named **Melandra** (SK 008951) just west of Glossop, is an example. This fort was occupied only between about AD 78 and 140 but excavations have revealed considerable ancillary buildings, including a bath house.

Other forts were at **Brough** *(Navio)* (SK 181828) in the Hope Valley and at **Chesterfield** and in the south there was a fort at **Little Chester** (SK 353376), a little to the north of the city centre of Derby. Little Chester was on **Ryknild Street**, a Roman road which ran through Burton-upon-Trent towards Yorkshire. There was a Roman road from Brough to Buxton and the road known as **Doctors Gate** joined the forts at Brough and Glossop. Many other traces of Roman roads are known and there have been numerous finds of such objects as pigs of lead, coins, altars, metalwork and pottery.

The extent to which the warm springs at **Buxton** *(Aquae Arnemetiae)* were utilised by the Romans is uncertain. At the most, such use seems to have been modest and far removed from the sophisticated establishment which existed at Bath.

ANGLO-SAXON PERIOD

The existence of barrows points to the continued occupation of the area after the end of the Roman period by the indigenous people, although such barrows are not numerous in comparison with other areas. The earthworks known as **Castle Hill** (SK 222688) on the east side of the Wye at Bakewell may have been the site of a large military camp of Edward the Elder, set up after he defeated the Danes in 924.

Outstanding among the monuments of Saxon Derbyshire is the crypt and chancel of the church at **Repton** (SK 304272), where there was one of the principal residences of the kings of Mercia. This is described in chapter 6.

There are Saxon crosses in a number of villages. The one at **Eyam** (SK 217764) is perhaps the best preserved whilst there are two at **Bakewell** (SK 216685). The Saxons also founded a town called Northworthy, which is known to us today as **Derby.**

MIDDLE AGES

Following the Norman conquest the greater part of Derbyshire and the Peak was subjected to forest laws, although this does not mean that any trees grew there. Followers of the king were granted the overlordship of vast areas and built castles to consolidate their holdings.

Peveril Castle, Castleton, Sheffield (map reference SK 149826). Telephone enquiries: Hope Valley (0433) 20613. *English Heritage.*

Peveril is the only castle in Derbyshire which presents any idea of what these Norman castles were like. The others have either largely disappeared as at Melbourne or been engulfed in later building as at Bolsover. The setting of Peveril Castle is all that could be desired in a castle, defended on two sides by precipices and with a curtain wall required only on the other two sides. The keep is of 1175 and traces have been found of the hall and ancillary buildings, although little else remains. The castle served as the centre for control of the Peak Forest and it was here in 1157 that Henry II met Malcolm of Scotland and received his allegiance. Sir Walter Scott gave an elaborated account of the event in *Peveril of the Peak.*

Peveril Castle.

19

St Oswald's church, Ashbourne, with its 212 foot high spire.

6
Churches and chapels

Derbyshire is not a county noted for an abundance of fine churches. In the Peak District there are few medieval churches as in the middle ages the area was formed into a few vast parishes and these were divided up only in the nineteenth century. Many of the churches are therefore of this latter period. The visitor to Derbyshire churches should be warned that many of them seem to be kept locked, with no notice displayed as to where a key may be obtained.

Ashbourne

The chancel is the oldest part of this fine cruciform town church, although there have been earlier churches on the site. The east window has glass by Kempe but the nave gives a curiously asymmetrical effect caused by the absence of a north aisle, which must have been intended when the rest of the church was built in the thirteenth century but was never built. The transepts are wide, with wide eastern aisles later adapted as the family chapels of the two local great families, the Bradbournes in the south transept and the Cockaynes, later Boothbys, in the north. The latter chapel contains the monument of 1791 to Penelope Boothby by Thomas Banks which brought fame to the sculptor, although the earlier

monuments of the Cockaynes are more important historically.

Bakewell

The large cruciform church of All Saints with its octagonal tower and spire dominates the little town and one has to walk uphill to the churchyard from Rutland Square. The church was heavily restored in the 1840s and 1850s, even to the extent of the nave being taken down and rebuilt, but remarkably the atmosphere of the church has survived this drastic treatment. The outstanding feature is the display of monuments in the large south transept known as the Newark. Here are the Vernon and Manners monuments of the families that built Haddon Hall. In the south aisle the alabaster monument of 1377 to Sir Godfrey Foljambe has Sir Godfrey and his wife looking out from a little balcony. There is an octagonal font of the early fourteenth century.

In the churchyard, a little to the south-east of the church, will be found a Saxon cross, some 8 feet (2.4 m) high, carved with scenes from the Passion and the Crucifixion. This is usually dated to about AD 750.

Chesterfield

The large cruciform church of All Saints is

20

mainly of the fourteenth century but the piers of the tower, the transepts and the eastern chapels survive from an earlier building. The profusion of chapels indicates that this is a great town church with each of the trade guilds having its own chapel. The Foljambe Chapel contains an important collection of alabaster monuments.

Gilbert Scott carried out a restoration in 1842-3, on the whole sensitively, and it does not strike the observer as virtually a Victorian church.

The feature for which this church is best known is the crooked spire; so famous has it become that it almost serves as a symbol for the town. The lead-covered timber spire has simply warped out of shape. It is 228 feet (69 m) high and leans over 9 feet (2.7 m) to the south-west, over 8 feet (2.4 m) to the south and nearly 4 feet (1.2 m) to the west.

Chinley

The Independent Chapel of 1667 (sometimes given as 1711) at Chapel Milton on A624 has two storeys of rectangular, mullioned windows, giving the building a domestic air. The interior is galleried and still has box pews and is thus a rare surviving example of the early nonconformist meeting house. The chapel is almost enveloped by enormous stone railway viaducts where three lines join at high level. The road passes far below at the side of the chapel.

Derby Cathedral

All Saints' church was promoted to the rank of cathedral in 1927 but as the principal parish church of Derby it has Saxon origins in a collegiate foundation. The earliest part of the present building is the magnificent west tower of the early sixteenth century; it still provides one of the main vertical features of the city centre when seen from afar.

By 1723 the remainder of the church was dilapidated and is said to have been demolished in the early hours of 18th February that year by order of the vicar, Dr Hutchinson. His action was intended to stir the townspeople into providing a replacement and in this it was successful, a new nave being built to designs by James Gibbs. The broad, vaulted interior is among the finest church interiors of the eighteenth century. The wrought iron screens to the chancel are by Robert Bakewell and are perhaps the greatest treasure of the cathedral.

Between 1967 and 1972 an extension to the east end was built, designed by Sebastian Comper. There is a baldachin of curious design over the high altar and beyond is a retrochoir. On a lower level are the chapter house, song school and offices. At the same time the cathedral was cleaned and redeco-

The skyline of Chesterfield is dominated by the famous crooked spire of the church of St Mary and All Saints.

rated so that it looks as bright and clean as it must have done to Bonnie Prince Charlie when he attended prayers here in 1745. There are engraved glass doors at the west end and excellent modern stained glass by Ceri Richards.

Hassop

The Roman Catholic church of All Saints stands close by the gates of Hassop Hall and was built between 1816 and 1818 to designs by Joseph Ireland for Anthony James Eyre, who had become Earl of Newburgh. The church is a classical temple and inside is a fine coffered ceiling and a large painting of the Crucifixion by Carracci.

Melbourne

Melbourne was granted to the Bishops of Carlisle by Henry I in 1133 on the foundation of that see and thus the church became of some importance, especially during the frequent intervals when the Bishop had to withdraw here when the Scots were threatening Carlisle.

The church is a Norman building of the grandest kind. Mainly of the twelfth century, although probably standing on older foundations, the central tower has been partly rebuilt. There are very low twin western towers, unprecedented in a parish church of this date. The external appearance of the building is not as impressive as it might be as the west front can hardly be seen because of a tithe barn standing only a few feet away. This, however, makes the interior all the more impressive for the massive columns of the nave arcade are 4 feet (1.2 m) in diameter and stand close together, giving a rather stilted appearance. The whole effect is similar to that of such great Norman churches as Durham or Ely cathedrals, albeit on a smaller scale.

Norbury

The noble church at Norbury stands close to the manor house in a picturesque group; indeed it almost seems to stand in the garden of the manor house. The south tower and nave were built in the fifteenth century by the Fitzherbert family, who also added the southwest chapel a little later. The glory of the church, however, is the chancel of the early fourteenth century, which is only a little shorter than the nave. The great windows still retain most of their original glass, now restored, and the impression of ancient splendour is unforgettable.

Steetley chapel, the south door with its elaborate Norman decoration.

Padley

Padley Hall was one of the numerous seats of the Eyre family, devoted Roman Catholics in times when it was dangerous to adhere to the church of Rome. The house was of the fourteenth and fifteenth centuries but the only remaining part is the chapel and what were once domestic offices below. These stood on the south side of the quadrangular house. Over the centuries the chapel declined to become a cowshed until, in 1932, the chapel was purchased and restored and reconsecrated as a Roman Catholic chapel in memory of two priests of the old faith who were found in the house and subsequently executed with great brutality in Derby in 1588. Two of the original doorways remain, with parts of the hammer-beam roof.

Repton

Repton has been a place of importance since the seventh century, when it became one of the bases of the kings of Mercia. There was a monastery here which was destroyed by the Danes and then a priory was founded in 1172. The church as it has come down to us is the result of a complicated series of alterations, the nave, aisles and western tower and spire being mainly work of the thirteenth and fourteenth centuries.

The chancel and its crypt are the most interesting parts of this church. The crypt was built as the burial place of King Ethelbert and of Wiglaf about AD 757. This crypt was later elaborated into a reliquary by the addition of four columns supporting a vaulted roof and then by the construction of two flights of steps leading down from the church above so that pilgrims could circulate around the holy relics. Here too St Wystan, grandson of Wiglaf, was buried. All this work seems to have been completed during the ninth century. The crypt at Repton is still being investigated but it is a fascinating experience to descend the stone stairs and to enter the world of the Saxons.

Saltersford

Isolated among the hills on the narrow road from Rainow to the Goyt Valley is the Jenkin Chapel (properly the church of St John). Built in 1733 with square windows of small panes, it is rather like a house save for the little tower with its pitched roof added in 1754. The interior retains the original fittings of box pews, pulpit and reading desk. The Jenkin Chapel reminds us of the great difficulties of providing places of worship in such sparsely populated hill country.

Steetley

In the far north-east of the county, just north of A619 and between Whitwell and Worksop, lies the chapel of the largely de-

Tideswell, the church of St John the Baptist visible above the roofs of the little town.

serted village of Steetley. The building was probably erected by Guy le Breton towards the end of the twelfth century. Although it is only 56 feet (17 m) long, there are a nave, chancel and apse all decorated with most elaborate carving; indeed it gives the impression of being almost a showplace of sculpture. The south doorway is also elaborately carved but much of this is due to the restoration carried out by J. L. Pearson in 1876-80 following a long period when the chapel was disused and roofless.

Tideswell

The church of St John the Baptist was built entirely in the fourteenth century in a remarkably co-ordinated manner for so large a church. The interior is impressive with its graceful arcades and the original fittings have been preserved to an unusual degree. There are many pre-reformation monuments. The tower was the last part of the church to be built and is in Perpendicular style. It forms a beautiful group with the village buildings, especially when seen from the narrow streets or from the hills which so closely surround Tideswell on every side.

Wirksworth

This large cruciform church has had several thorough restorations, the last by Scott in the 1870s. The oldest parts of the building are thirteenth-century but sculptured fragments from an earlier building are built into the present one. These may be Norman, possibly Saxon. In those times Wirksworth was a dependency of Repton. What is probably a coffin lid of about AD 800 is built into the north wall and may have come from the tomb of a saint or other important person. It shows biblical scenes. The remainder of the building dates from the thirteenth to fifteenth centuries, although the nineteenth century contributed much, including the eastern aisles of the transepts, which were enlarged in 1820 to take galleries and then altered to look more medieval by Scott.

The spiky spire on the tower is attractive and the church stands in its churchyard, which is secluded from the streets of the little town almost like a miniature cathedral close.

Youlgreave

The massive Perpendicular tower of this church dominates the large one-street village. The Norman nave, with its round columns, is the main feature of interest inside. Windows have fine nineteenth-century glass, especially that of the east window, designed by Burne-Jones and made by William Morris in 1876. The restoration of 1869-70 was by Norman Shaw, an architect not noted for such work, but was mostly of a sensitive nature.

23

Bolsover Castle, the terrace range of long-ruined great rooms with their 'cannon' buttresses.

Historic houses and gardens

Bolsover Castle, Bolsover, Chesterfield. Telephone enquiries: Chesterfield (0246) 823349. *English Heritage.*

Little remains of the twelfth-century castle at Bolsover, the present extraordinary assemblage of buildings dating from the seventeenth century and dominating from its crag the landscape of collieries, heavy industry and the M1 motorway.

Sir Charles Cavendish, son of Bess of Hardwick, acquired the castle in 1613 from his stepbrother, the seventh Earl of Shrewsbury, and commenced building. Sir Charles's son, the first Duke of Newcastle, built the great range of rooms, long roofless, along the edge of the cliff for a visit of Charles I in 1634, when the king heard a masque, *Love's Welcome* by Ben Jonson. He also built the range along the other side of the great court, with the Riding School and its attendant forge and harness rooms.

The walled enclosure of the medieval castle was retained and made into the Fountain Garden with a Venus fountain. The keep, or Little Castle, was built by Sir Charles as virtually a separate dwelling and this remains entire. To visit these quite small rooms, elaborately decorated in a Jacobean style, with much use of allegory, is among the strangest of architectural experiences. The designers of all these buildings seem to have been members of the Smythson family, Robert, John and Huntingdon Smythson, who were kept busy at Bolsover until 1640.

Calke Abbey, Ticknal, Derby DE7 1LE. Telephone enquiries: Derby (0332) 863822. 2 miles (3 km) south-west of Melbourne. *National Trust.*

Calke Abbey is a great house hitherto unknown to the public but which has acquired fame during the successful struggle to save it for the nation.

The house stands on the site of an Augustinian priory and was built between 1701 and 1703 for Sir John Harpur on the grandest scale. Alterations were subsequently carried out but the latest appear to be the addition of the portico in the 1800s and a number of interior remodellings. Both the buildings and its contents have remained remarkably untouched since then and the house has been virtually inaccessible to the public.

The house stands in a fine park and there are stables of 1712-16. An avenue of limes leads to the house and what at first appears to be a lake is part of Staunton Harold Reservoir, which adds to the beauty of the place.

24

Chatsworth, Bakewell DE4 1PP. Telephone: Baslow (024 688) 2204. The Baslow to Matlock road, B6012, passes through the park. *Chatsworth House Trust.*

Chatsworth is one of the most famous houses in England, and seat of the Dukes of Devonshire. The present house, replacing one of Elizabethan times, was built between 1687 and 1707 and extended in 1820-42. The splendours of classical architecture are enriched by the greatest art collection in private hands in Britain, with paintings, sculpture and a magnificent library. Chatsworth is no place for a hurried visit.

But the outstanding feature of Chatsworth is the setting. The gardens are among the most spectacular in Europe. The great Cascade, many fountains, long vistas and seemingly natural but really artificial rocks are there to delight the visitor. There is an arboretum of exotic trees and the whole is set in a park of undulating grassland between hills clothed in hanging woodlands, whilst the rushing waters of the Derwent have been dammed to form a stately river suitable to the location.

The park is surrounded by a series of estate villages of which **Edensor** (pronounced Ensor) is of particular interest. It was built about 1839 to replace the old village, which was too near the Duke's windows. The houses display an extraordinary collection of fanciful architectural styles, which yet contrive to harmonise with each other in an attractive way. The village was probably planned by Sir Joseph Paxton, head gardener to the Duke, who shortly afterwards achieved fame as the designer of the Crystal Palace for the Great Exhibition in Hyde Park in 1851.

Elvaston Castle. See chapter 3, under 'Country parks'.

Haddon Hall, Bakewell DE4 1LA. Telephone: Bakewell (062 981) 2855. 2 miles (3 km) south of Bakewell, entrance off A6. *The Duke of Rutland.*

Only a few miles from Chatsworth is Haddon Hall, residence of the Dukes of Rutland. Dating from many periods between the twelfth and sixteenth centuries, Haddon is an irregular, yet supremely satisfying complex of building. Much smaller than its august neighbour, it is an amazingly well preserved house and shows us what we should all like to think of as a medieval house. Turrets and battlements abound in a great show of defence, yet beneath them large mullioned windows look out across green velvet lawns to the woods within which Haddon lies.

The river Wye contributes much to the incomparable setting of Haddon Hall and the house stands on a grassy eminence with the buildings seeming almost to grow out of the ground, so perfectly is the architecture suited to the site.

Hardwick Hall, Doe Lea, Chesterfield S44 5QJ. Telephone: Chesterfield (0246) 850430. 9 miles (15 km) south-east of Chesterfield, approached by signposted turnings off A617. *National Trust.*

Hardwick Hall crowns a hilltop, displaying its towers to those passing by along the M1 motorway in the valley below. It was created by that proud and able woman Bess of Hardwick. She was born the daughter of the modest manor house in about 1520. It was only

Chatsworth House, from the east.

CHAPTER 7

Kedleston Hall, south front.

after she had separated from her fourth and richest husband, the sixth Earl of Shrewsbury, that she felt free to give full rein to her passion for building and she began by enlarging the old manor house, now known as the Old Hall and in ruins. Through the gaping windows one can see the remains of plasterwork decorations although the work was never finished.

The Earl died in 1590, when Bess was about seventy years of age, and she was then able to use her wealth as well as her own. She decided to build an entirely new hall, close to the old one, but to the most up-to-date design, probably by Robert Smythson. The suite of state rooms is on the second floor, approached by a carefully calculated series of flights of steps from the great hall in the centre of the ground floor. The private apartments were on the first floor with the service quarters on either side of the hall on the ground floor. The heights of each floor reflect this progression, the top floor being the tallest, and from the vast windows of the Long Gallery and the High Great Chamber one looks down to the walled gardens, which have retained their original layout of crenellated walls.

Bess died in 1608 and her descendants rose higher to create even greater houses such as Chatsworth. Hardwick became a secondary residence, little used through the eighteenth century, until early in the following century the sixth Duke of Devonshire realised the antiquarian interest of the old house.

There is much fine furniture and the tapestries are notable. The hunting scenes in plasterwork are supremely characteristic of the age which built this house.

For Hardwick Hall Country Park see chapter 3.

Heights of Abraham, Matlock Bath, Matlock. Telephone: Matlock (0629) 582365.

The land on the slopes of Masson Hill was enclosed in 1780 and shortly afterwards zig-zag paths were made so that visitors could admire the spectacular scenery. Formerly there had been lead mines here and the old workings were opened for visitors early in the nineteenth century. Many trees were planted about the same time. The result seems to have been a 'savage' or 'alpine' garden intended from the start as a commercial tourist attraction, which it continues to be. Access has always been a problem as the steep approach roads are narrow, with no possibility of a car park. This problem has been solved by a cable car system, which carries visitors across the gorge of the Derwent from a car park close to Matlock Bath station. The name derives from the Heights of Abraham scaled by the troops of General Wolfe near Quebec in 1759.

Kedleston Hall, Kedleston, Quarndon, Derby DE6 4JN. Telephone: Derby (0322) 842191. 4 miles (6 km) north-west of Derby on the minor road to Hulland. *National Trust.*

Kedleston Hall is the outstanding Georgian house in Derbyshire and the work of three of the greatest architects of the age. Matthew Brettingham was responsible for the general plan of a central block of state rooms with pavilions connected by quadrant corridors. He began by building the north-east pavilion as private quarters for Sir Nathaniel Curzon (later the first Lord Scarsdale). There had been an earlier house on the site, barely forty years old, but this was demolished and the main central block built between 1760 and 1765 along with the north-west pavilion containing the kitchens. This was supervised by James Paine, who also seems to have revised the designs for the main block. By 1760 a third architect had taken full charge of the work. He was Robert Adam and it is his distinctive mark which is dominant at Kedleston, especially in the interior.

The hall, with its ranks of alabaster columns, overwhelms one with the magnificence of the house as one enters the door. As one progresses through the state rooms, each varied in character, one can appreciate not only the splendour of the design but also the care taken over every detail, even to the elegant radiators in the saloon.

On the ground floor is a display of memorabilia of Marquess Curzon of Kedleston, Viceroy of India from 1898-1905, the most notable member of the family. The house stands in the midst of a great landscape park also designed by Adam and there are attractive gardens.

Lea Rhododendron Gardens, Lea, Matlock. Telephone: Dethick (062 984) 380. 5 miles (8 km) south-east of Matlock, off B6024. *Mr and Mrs Tye.*

Although these gardens are only 2½ acres (1.0 ha) in extent, they appear much larger as a network of paths meanders about this former gritstone quarry, among the magnificent rhododendrons. The garden was started by Mr J. B. Marsden-Smedley in 1935, taking advantage of the light shade provided by silver birch and Scots pine planted early in the twentieth century. There are some five hundred different rhododendrons in these gardens and plants are sold to visitors.

Lyme Park, Disley, Stockport, Cheshire SK12 2NX. Telephone: New Mills (0663) 62023. Entrance to the park just west of Disley on A6. *National Trust, managed by Stockport Metropolitan Borough Council.*

For six hundred years Lyme Park was owned by the Legh family, from whom it passed to the National Trust in 1947. Of Elizabethan origin, the house owes its present form to alterations and enlargements by Giacomo Leoni in 1726 and further enlarge-

ments by Lewis Wyatt in 1817. Leoni designed the portico overlooking the small lake on the south front and his interiors are mainly along this side of the house. The staircase and the saloon are especially fine. A good deal of Elizabethan work remains, including the Long Gallery and the Drawing Room. The park is now a country park (see chapter 3).

Melbourne Hall, Melbourne, Derby DE7 1EN. Telephone: Melbourne (033 16) 2502. 8 miles (13 km) south of Derby, close to the church. *Lord Kerr.*

The house is beautifully situated by Melbourne Pool with its famous garden entirely to the east. Parts of the house date back to the thirteenth century, when the hall was a residence of the Bishops of Carlisle. The house was leased in 1629 by Sir John Coke, Secretary to Charles I, and further parts of the house date from this time. In the eighteenth century numerous alterations and extensions were made, including the east front of 1744. This is the garden front and the only facade that sets out to impress the observer in any way.

The wrought iron arbour, known as the Birdcage, in the gardens of Melbourne Hall, made by Robert Bakewell.

Sudbury Hall, the south or garden front.

Melbourne Hall is a pleasant, habitable house with fine panelling and furniture and attractive family pictures.

The garden is, however, the great feature of Melbourne Hall. Towards the end of the seventeenth century Colonel Coke, grandson of Sir John, began to enlarge the original small garden and planted the yew tunnel as a covered walk, which still exists. The main development of the garden is due to the Colonel's son, Thomas Coke, who, after 1696, gradually expanded his ideas until he had made the magnificent formal garden leading down to the pool and culminating in the wrought iron arbour made by the local smith, Robert Bakewell, in 1706. This part of the garden was designed under the supervision of London and Wise, the outstanding garden designers of the age. Further south is another section of the garden, which seems to have been laid out at about the same time, with long, hedged walks crossing at pools where fountains play. The main walk leads uphill to the great Four Seasons Vase, said to have been presented to Thomas Coke by Queen Anne, whose Vice Chamberlain he had become.

Sudbury Hall, Sudbury, Derby DE6 5HT. Telephone: Sudbury (028 378) 305. Off the Derby to Uttoxeter road, A50, where it is crossed by the A515. *National Trust.*

The approach to Sudbury Hall, standing

back from the road and now bypassed by the A50, prepares one for something special and few visitors will be disappointed. The Vernon family owned Sudbury from 1513 and it was George Vernon who built the present house in the 1660s and 1670s. He is likely to have acted as his own architect for there are a number of features which must have been very old-fashioned in Restoration England. Both inside and out it is remarkably little changed and Sudbury is most famous for its interior decoration. A good deal of the work was done by local men but for some of it Vernon called on the leading London craftsmen of the day. Carving was done by Grinling Gibbons and Edward Pearce, and stucco work by Bradbury and Pettifer.

The long gallery on the top floor is a splendid room, with its ceiling by Bradbury and Pettifer, even though the idea of a long gallery was outmoded when it was built. The staircase is in the richest taste of the period but it is perhaps the saloon that is the most imposing room in this splendid house.

To the south an informally planted garden slopes down to a small lake. This was designed, at least in its outline, by William Sawrey Gilpin, although the origin of the lake is earlier. The terraces before the house date from 1837 and the flower beds were laid out by the National Trust, which took over the house in 1967, to emphasise the Victorian character of the garden. To the north of the house most of the park is not owned by the Trust and is not accessible to visitors; it lies on the other side of the main road. From the upper floor of the house one nevertheless has a good view of the park and especially of the curious deercote, which looks rather like a toy fort. This dates from 1723 but was later elaborated to make an ornamental feature of the park.

The museum in the nineteenth-century wing is managed by the county council separately from the house (see chapter 8).

Sutton Scarsdale, Chesterfield. 4 miles (6 km) east of Chesterfield, approached by a minor road between Arkwright Town on A632 and Heath on A617. *English Heritage.* The exterior can be seen at any reasonable time.

The house is seventeenth-century in origin but was largely remodelled by Francis Smith of Warwick in 1724 for Nicholas Leeke, second Earl of Scarsdale. The main facade is to the east, with the entrance to the north. Early in the nineteenth century the property was bought by the Arkwrights, but it was abandoned in the 1920s. Many of the interior fittings were sold and they may be seen now at Philadelphia in the United States. The shell of the house was left to decay amid encroaching vegetation, whilst all around opencast coal mining devastated the landscape. However, shortly after the Second World War Sir Osbert Sitwell bought the ruins to preserve what was left. English Heritage has consolidated the walls to prevent further decay and cleared away the vegetation. The opencast mining has ceased and the surrounding land has been restored. Something of the melancholy beauty has been lost but Sutton Scarsdale will survive to remind us what riches may be lost by apathetic neglect.

Sutton Scarsdale Hall. The ruins are now in the care of English Heritage.

Revolution House, Old Whittington, Chesterfield.

8
Museums

BAKEWELL
Old House Museum, Cunningham Place, Bakewell DE4 1DD. Telephone: Bakewell (062981) 3647. *Bakewell and District Historical Society.*

This is a folk museum displaying craftsmen's tools, Victorian kitchen, costumes, toys and lacework and the building housing the museum is at least as important as the contents. The Old House is close to the church and was originally the parsonage house. It was built in about 1534 although subsequently passing through a complicated series of alterations and extensions. During the eighteenth century it was leased to Sir Richard Arkwright, who turned it into tenements for employees of his cotton mill. In 1954 the building was taken over by its present owners and restored as a museum.

BUXTON
Buxton Museum and Art Gallery, Terrace Road, Buxton SK17 6DU. Telephone: Buxton (0298) 4658. *Derbyshire County Council.* This is a small museum displaying material from the locality including archaeological finds discovered in the course of quarrying. The geological collection is notable, with objects of Blue John and black Ashford marble. There

are relics of the High Peak Railway. The art gallery on the first floor has an interesting collection of pictures relating to the early history of Buxton.

CASTLETON
Cavendish House Museum, Cavendish House, Cross Street, Castleton, Sheffield S30 2WH. Telephone: Hope Valley (0433) 20642.

The Ollerenshaw Collection is a private museum of Blue John, porcelain and items of geological interest.

CHESTERFIELD
Revolution House, High Street, Old Whittington, Chesterfield S41 9LA. Telephone: Chesterfield (0246) 35928. 2½ miles (4 km) north of the town centre, on B6052. *Chesterfield Borough Council.*

The Revolution House is the remaining fragment of the Cock and Pynot inn and owes its fame to events in 1688. It was in this building that the fourth Earl of Devonshire, the Earl of Danby and John D'Arcy, heir to the Earl of Holderness, met to plan the invitation to William of Orange to take the crown in place of the hated James II. Thus the Glorious Revolution, which culminated in November 1688 when William landed at Torbay, was plotted in this obscure wayside inn. The humble nature of the place was doubtless an advantage in maintaining secrecy.

The building continued to be used as an inn until long after the first centenary celebrations in 1788, although it was already becoming known as the Revolution House. Later it became a cottage, a new inn being built alongside which still stands and carries the old name in a modernised form, the Cock and Magpie. Parts of the old building were demolished but some repairs were carried out for the 1888 celebrations. The 250th anniversary was celebrated by the opening of the building to the public as a museum.

The interior is furnished in the manner of the late seventeenth century and there is a copy of the 'Plotting Chair' in which the Earl of Devonshire is said to have sat (the original is at Hardwick Hall). There is a collection of documents relating to the events of 1688, some of which are displayed on the first floor.

CRICH

National Tramway Museum, Crich, Matlock DE4 5DP. Telephone: Ambergate (077 385) 2565. 6 miles (10 km) south-east of Matlock, north of Crich. *Tramway Museum Society.*

The origin of this most unusual museum was a large limestone quarry operated by the railway pioneer George Stephenson, who built a narrow gauge railway to link the quarry to his main line at Ambergate. The route of this narrow gauge line has been adapted as a tramway, about 1 mile (1.6 km) long.

The collection of tramcars, formed since 1959, includes some forty vehicles from all manner of tramway systems, British and foreign. About one third of the collection is in working order and these vehicles provide rides for visitors. There is an urban street setting giving the atmosphere of the late Victorian and Edwardian period, when tramcars were in their heyday, and notable among the buildings is the facade of the old Derby Assembly Rooms of 1774, damaged by fire in 1963 and re-erected here. A bandstand and gas lamps add to the period scene. About half way along the route is a display by the Peak District Mines Historical Society for Crich was formerly a centre of the lead-mining industry.

There is an exhibition on tramcars and occasionally in the autumn there are evening openings, when the trams and the street are illuminated. The museum provides a rare opportunity to experience a type of public transport now almost extinct.

DERBY

Derby Industrial Museum, The Silk Mill, Silk Mill Lane, off Full Street, Derby DE1 3AR. Telephone: Derby (0332) 293111 extension 740. *Derby City Council.*

The Silk Mill was built between 1717 and 1721 by George Sorocold for Thomas Lombe. The mill was equipped with machines for the doubling, or twisting, of silk into silk thread. An undershot waterwheel provided power from the adjoining river Derwent. In 1908 the association with the silk industry ended and in 1910 the mill was burnt out and the east wall collapsed into the river. Rebuilding retained the essential features of the mill but, although the height of the rebuilt mill is the same as the original, there are three tall storeys as opposed to the earlier five low storeys. The distinctive tower is much the same as formerly.

The building became the Derby Industrial Museum in 1974 and few such museums can be more appropriately housed, as this building was the prototype for all subsequent textile factory buildings. On the ground floor are exhibits relating to Rolls-Royce aero engines, a local industry since 1915. On the first floor are general displays on Derbyshire industries including lead and coal mining, ironfounding, limestone quarrying and brickmaking. The adjoining Sowter Mill has been renovated and

The Silk Mill, Derby Industrial Museum.

The Joseph Wright gallery, a part of the Derby City Art Gallery.

there are plans for extensions to include engineering, especially railway engineering, and the development of the local textile industry.

Derby Museum and Art Gallery, The Strand, Derby DE1 1BS. Telephone: Derby (0332) 293111, extension 782. *Derby City Council.*

Like many similar institutions, Derby Museum had its origin in several collections formed by learned societies in the town and in Derby these were taken over by the council in 1870. The oldest part of the present building is that fronting the Wardwick and which has the public library on the ground floor. This was built in 1879 and various extensions followed, partly to accommodate the art gallery. The 1964 extension now provides the entrance and several attractive display galleries.

The ground-floor gallery close to the entrance houses a magnificent collection of Derby porcelain from the mid eighteenth century to the present. There are archaeological displays on the origins of man in Derbyshire and of Roman objects from the site of the fort at Little Chester to the north of the city centre. A remarkable object of Anglo-Saxon date is the sarcophagus of St Alkmund, discovered during excavations on the site of the church of St Alkmund, demolished to build a ring road.

There is a large natural history gallery, from which one may enter the Joseph Wright gallery, which contains the major collection of paintings by this important local artist, who is increasingly recognised as of international importance. There are further galleries devoted to temporary exhibitions, some of which draw on the reserve collections, which include many pictures of old Derby and Derbyshire.

The coin display includes coins minted in Derby between 940 and 1154 and there is a large gallery devoted to military history. There are galleries of geology and of the social history of Derby. An unusual feature is the large model of the Midland Railway and adjoining is the Frank Bradley collection of toy theatres.

There are two reconstructions of whole rooms in the museum. One of these is the saloon bar of a public house of the early twentieth century, which has been fitted up by using material from two old Derby pubs. It is complete with glasses and bottles and occasionally this museum object comes to life when the Friends of the Museum and Art Gallery gather to ensure that the glasses do not gather too much dust. The other room reconstruction is one removed from Exeter House, demolished in the mid nineteenth century, and is the room in which Bonnie Prince Charlie held his fateful conference with his generals at which he decided to retreat to Scotland, and Culloden, during the 1745 rebellion.

Pickford's House Museum, 41 Friargate, Derby DE1 1DA. Telephone: Derby (0332) 293111, extension 402 or 782. *Derby City Council.*

Pickford's House is named in honour of Joseph Pickford, the outstanding Derby architect of the late eighteenth century. 41 Friargate was built by Pickford in 1770 for himself and incorporates drawing instruments in the decoration above the front door. The house is now a museum of social history with rooms furnished to show life in Derby at various periods over the last two hundred years. There is also a display on Friargate and vicinity.

Royal Crown Derby Museum, Osmaston Road, Derby DE3 8JZ. Telephone: Derby (0332) 47051. *Royal Crown Derby Porcelain Company Ltd.*

The origins of porcelain manufacture in Derby are obscure but Andrew Planché seems to have commenced making porcelain in the early 1750s. The early production was almost entirely of figures, very little tableware being known from this period. In 1756 Planché entered into partnership with John Heath, a banker, and William Duesbury, an enameller, and they opened a factory on Nottingham Road which produced a much greater range of products. Duesbury later became the dominant partner, opening a showroom in London in 1775, and royal patronage was accorded for the first time. After Duesbury's death in 1786 the business passed to his son, also William, usually known as Duesbury II. Under his management the Derby factory achieved European fame and had an outstanding group of craftsmen and painters.

There seems to have been a decline following the early death of Duesbury II in 1797 but in 1811 Robert Bloor took over and the business revived somewhat, but before his death in 1846 management was poor and in 1848 the factory was sold. Some of the potters and painters then began their own business at a factory in King Street.

In 1875 the Derby Crown Porcelain Company was formed with a factory incorporating the buildings of the old Derby Union Workhouse, built in 1839, and this remains the factory today. This attractive museum is on the first floor of the front block of the factory, facing Osmaston Road, and was opened in 1969. There are displays of all periods of production, including the present, and china manufacture continues in adjoining buildings.

ELVASTON
Elvaston Working Estate Museum. See chapter 3, under 'Country parks'.

EYAM
Eyam Private Museum, The Lydgate, Eyam, Sheffield. Telephone: Hope Valley (0433) 31010. *Mr Clarence Daniel.*

This is a private museum on the history and topography of the 'plague' village of Eyam, and visitors are welcome by appointment.

The Kedleston Vase, in the Royal Crown Derby Museum, was commissioned by Lord Scarsdale around 1790. The snake handles were modelled by Jean Jacques Spangler. One panel, 'Virgins awakening Cupid' was by James Bamford; the other is a view of Kedleston Hall by Zachariah Boreman, while the swags of pink roses were painted by William Billingsley.

ILKESTON

Erewash Museum, High Street, Ilkeston. Telephone: Ilkeston (0602) 440440, extension 331. *Erewash Borough Council.*

This new museum occupies a late eighteenth-century house on a minor turning to the east of St Mary's church and looks out eastwards across a pleasant garden towards the Erewash valley. The displays are mainly of local interest relating to the Erewash district, which includes Long Eaton as well as Ilkeston. There are displays of lacemaking and other local industries, room reconstructions and costume displays.

LONGNOR

Folk Museum, Longnor, Buxton. Opening times may be obtained from any National Park Information Centre.

A small village museum is housed in the Methodist church.

MATLOCK BATH

Matlock Bath Model Railway Museum, Temple Road, Matlock Bath, Matlock DE4 3PG. Telephone: Matlock (0629) 2282.

This is a model of Derbyshire railways.

Peak District Mining Museum, The Pavilion, Matlock Bath, Matlock. Telephone: Matlock (0629) 3834.

This museum is housed in the Pavilion, which was built about 1906 as the social centre of the resort. The building has been restored and opened as a museum of the mining industry of the area. The centrepiece is the water pressure engine of 1819, which was recovered by members of the Peak District Mines Historical Society from a depth of 360 feet (110 m) in a mine at Winster. There are displays of tools and other mining equipment, all in a setting which endeavours to recreate the atmosphere of an old lead mine.

SUDBURY

Museum of Childhood, Sudbury Hall, Sudbury, Derby DE6 5HT. Telephone: Sudbury (028 378) 305. *Derbyshire County Council.*

This museum occupies the nineteenth-century service wing of Sudbury Hall (for the hall see chapter 7), together with the seventeenth-century stable block, and is managed by the county council in association with the National Trust, which owns all the buildings and manages the hall and gardens.

The museum displays the life of children, mainly in the nineteenth and early twentieth centuries, but with some material from earlier periods. There is an Edwardian nursery, toy room, costume corridor, Victorian parlour and Edwardian schoolroom, besides displays on the life of children during the Second World War. The emphasis is on things young visitors can do for themselves and there is a chimney to climb and a mine tunnel to crawl through.

Apart from the Museum of Childhood the Sudbury Hall museum has a permanent collection of modern ceramics and there are frequent temporary exhibitions.

The Pavilion at Matlock Bath, now housing the tourist information centre and the Peak District Mining Museum.

Cromford Wharf, the end of the Cromford Canal.

9
Other places to visit

BUXTON

Buxton Micrarium, The Crescent, Buxton SK17 6BQ. Telephone: Buxton (0298) 78662.

Buxton Micrarium is the first 'Planetarium of the Microscope' and is unique in the world.

Special microscopes, with push button controls for the visitor to operate, project images of specimens drawn from the whole of the natural world on to television size screens.

Peak Rail, Midland Railway Station site, Buxton. Telephone enquiries: Buxton (0298) 79898.

A collection of steam and diesel locomotives is located next to the present British Rail station. Short passenger rides are sometimes given. Part of the collection is located near the railway station at Matlock.

CROMFORD

Cromford Canal, Old Wharf, Mill Lane, Cromford, Matlock. Telephone: Wirksworth (062 982) 3727. *Cromford Canal Society.*

The canal was completed by 1793 and linked the Erewash Canal at Langley Mill with Cromford. Richard Arkwright was one of the promoters of the project although he died before it was operational. Through traffic ended in 1900 with the collapse of the Butterley Tunnel and the section from Cromford to Ambergate was purchased by the county council in 1974 for leisure use. The section from Cromford to Leawood aqueduct has been restored by the Cromford Canal Society. There is a steam museum at Cromford Wharf. The Leawood Pumphouse is open to the public and regularly 'in steam' and there are horse-drawn passenger boats on the canal.

Cromford Mill, Mill Lane, Cromford, Matlock. Telephone: Wirksworth (062 982) 4297. *Arkwright Society.*

This is the water-powered mill built by Richard Arkwright when he moved from Nottingham to Cromford in 1771. It is the earliest factory building for spinning cotton in the world. Cotton spinning was in decline here by about 1840 and the buildings were leased for other purposes such as a brewery and, most recently, a colour works.

In 1979 the Arkwright Society purchased the mill with a view to restoring the buildings. This work is still in progress but already the site is open to the public and there is an exhibition on spinning and weaving and on Arkwright and his project at Cromford. There is a room reconstruction of a worker's cottage with its knitting frame. Guided tours of the mill and the village can be arranged.

Cromford and High Peak Railway Workshops. Lea Bridge, Cromford. Telephone: Wirksworth (062982) 2831. *Derbyshire County Council.* About 1½ miles from Cromford, signposted from the Cromford to Crich road.

The original workshops of this pioneering

35

railway (see page 12) with the forge with hand bellows, a section of the track still in place and an audio-visual programme.

GLOSSOP

Dinting Railway Centre, Dinting Lane, Glossop. Telephone: Glossop (045 74) 5596. About 1 mile (1.6 km) west of the centre of Glossop on A57.

This is a collection of locomotives, regularly in steam, offering free brake van rides.

ILKESTON

The American Adventure, PO Box 1, Ilkeston, Derbyshire DE7 5SX. On the A6007 road between Ilkeston and Heanor. Telephone: Ilkeston (0773) 769931. *Park Hall Leisure.*

An American theme park offers over a hundred themed attractions including Thunder Canyon, the highest Log Flume in Britain. The Santa Fé railway connects the Indian Reservation, Niagara Rapids and Pioneer Playland, an undercover area for children's fun and games with cartoon cinema. Silver City has daily shoot-outs between the Sheriff, his Deputies and Bandits. Space Port USA simulates space travel.

MATLOCK BATH

Gulliver's Kingdom, Temple Walk, Matlock Bath, Matlock DE4 3PG. Telephone: Matlock (0629) 55970.

There is a model village and a dinosaur park in the woods.

MIDDLETON-BY-WIRKSWORTH

Middleton Top Engine House, Middleton, Derby. Telephone: Wirksworth (062 982) 3204. *Derbyshire County Council.*

This twin beam winding engine was built by the Butterley Company in 1829 to haul wagons up the 1 in 8¼ Middleton Incline on the Cromford and High Peak Railway. The sole survivor of nine that worked on the line, it ceased working in 1963 and is being restored by volunteers. The engine house is regularly open and 'in steam'. Adjoining is a visitor centre and picnic site and there are cycles for hire to those who wish to cycle along the High Peak Trail (see chapter 3).

RIBER

Riber Castle Wildlife Park, Riber Castle, Matlock DE4 5JU. Telephone: Matlock (0629) 2073. South-east of Matlock, best reached by the minor road turning south off B6014 at Tansley. *Fauna Reserve (Riber) Ltd.*

Riber Castle is a conspicuous landmark on its hill above Matlock, built between 1862 and 1868 by Joseph Smedley. It now houses a collection of British and European birds and animals. The collection of lynx is notable but there are also vultures, wallabies, eagles and others as well as rare breeds of domesticated creatures.

In addition to the animal and bird collections, there are displays of vintage cars and motorcycles as well as a children's playground and a model railway.

RIPLEY

Midland Railway Centre, Butterley Station, Ripley, Derby DE5 3TL. Telephone: Ripley (0773) 47674. *Midland Railway Trust.*

Derby was the headquarters of the Midland Railway and this Centre serves as a permanent memorial to one of the great railway companies of Britain. The museum is still in course of development but there are some 3 miles (5 km) of working track from Hammersmith to Swanwick Junction, where the museum building is located, and to Ironville. The earliest locomotive dates from 1866 but there are diesels of 1959.

ROWSLEY

Caudwell's Mill, Rowsley, Matlock DE4 2EB. Telephone: Matlock (0629) 734374.

This stone-built flour mill is powered by water turbines first installed in 1885. Closed in 1978, it has been restored by volunteers and again produces wholemeal flour. There is an exhibition on the history of milling.

WIRKSWORTH

National Stone Centre, Ravenstor Road, Wirksworth DE4 4FR. Telephone: Matlock (0629) 824833. 1 mile north of Wirksworth off B5035.

Here the story of stones is told from its origins in coral seas, deltas and volcanoes to its use in products ranging from sugar to silica chips. The centre is being developed as a major focus for the display and interpretation of past and present stone quarrying and processing industries.

The beam engine house at Watt's Shaft, Mill Close Mine.

10
Mines and quarries

LEAD MINING

Among the most important activities in Derbyshire in the past was the production of lead from the ores which occur throughout the limestone area but especially in the Castleton, Eyam and Matlock areas. The ore is found as galena (lead sulphide), along with a number of other minerals, in long vertical fissures, known as rakes, which often run across country for many miles. Whilst the first workings would have been simple quarrying of the ores which occurred on the surface, mining seems to have begun at an early date.

The lead miners had an elaborate code of customs under which the finder of lead ore was entitled to enough land and water from the landowner to enable him to work his find. First he had to present a dish of lead ore to the Barmaster, the official of the Barmote, which regulated the industry.

The Romans were attracted to the Peak District by the lead obtainable and it was a valuable product throughout the middle ages. Production rose to its highest point during the eighteenth century, when it was an important export, and serious decline did not set in until after 1850. Some lead is still produced in the Peak, a mine near Matlock Bath being active in exploiting old workings.

The minerals associated with lead, mainly fluorspar, barytes and calcite, were thrown out as waste by the old miners but today these have become valuable for many industrial purposes. Numerous abandoned spoil heaps are being worked over again and the modern lead miners are finding the other minerals more valuable than the lead.

Lead mining has left conspicuous marks upon many parts of the limestone country. The lead rakes can be clearly traced in many places running across the landscape as a line of disturbed ground, usually grassed over but often planted with trees to prevent animals being poisoned by the lead in the soil. Many fields are pitted with the shallow depressions of old workings and traces of lead smelting are still to be seen here and there.

The visitor today may also see the modern successors of the old miners at work. In some corner of a field one or two men may be seen turning over old spoil heaps to recover the associated minerals once tipped there as waste.

CAVERNS OPEN TO THE PUBLIC

The long history of lead mining has left many disused workings and some of these, as well as some natural caves, have been made accessible to the public. The following caverns are now open to the public:

Bagshawe Cavern, Bradwell, Sheffield. Telephone: Hope Valley (0433) 20540.

CHAPTER 10

Blue John Cavern, Mam Tor, Castleton, Sheffield. Telephone: Hope Valley (0433) 20638.

Great Rutland Cavern and Nestus Mine, Matlock Bath, Matlock. Within the grounds of the Heights of Abraham, see chapter 7.

Holme Bank Chert Mine, Bakewell. Telephone: Chesterfield (0246) 75461.

Peak Cavern, Castleton, Sheffield. Telephone: Hope Valley (0433) 20285.

Poole's Cavern, Green Lane, Buxton. In Buxton Country Park, see chapter 3.

Royal Cave, Temple Walk, Matlock Bath, Matlock DE14 3PG. Telephone: Matlock (0629) 55970 or 3654.

Speedwell Cavern, Winnats Pass, Castleton, Sheffield S30 2WA. Telephone: Hope Valley (0433) 20512.

Temple Mine, Matlock Bath, Matlock. Associated with the Peak District Mining Museum, Matlock Bath, see chapter 8.

Treak Cliff Cavern, Castleton, Sheffield S30 2WP. Telephone: Hope Valley (0433) 20571.

Millstones abandoned in a quarry near Grindleford.

QUARRYING

In parts of the Peak District there are a great many quarries, some of them very large. They are most conspicuous in the limestone area, particularly near Buxton and to a lesser extent near Stoney Middleton, Matlock and Wirksworth.

Limestone was formerly worked mainly for burning to produce lime for agriculture and building, and Buxton lime is still famous. Today production is mainly for supply to the chemical industry, although much still reaches the farmer and builder. The industry has undergone a thorough process of concentration, the number of quarries being drastically reduced, whilst output has soared as more sophisticated plant has been installed.

The industry is concentrated in certain parts of the Peak because in those areas the limestone is particularly pure and this is important for the chemical industry.

Gritstone was formerly worked extensively for building stone, thin slabs being used for roofing. Because of the high cost of building in gritstone, however, this use has almost ceased, even the well known stone from Stancliffe, Darley Dale, from which many famous buildings all over England were built, being now in little demand. Millstones were once a common product of gritstone quarrying; indeed the stone is often referred to as the millstone grit. Cheaper means are now used to provide grindstones but abandoned millstones can be seen in a number of old quarries and some have even found a new use, mounted upon stone pedestals, as an appropriate sign at the entrances to the national park.

Two distinctive kinds of limestone are those of Hopton Wood near Wirksworth, which is in demand for decorative interior building work, and the so called Derbyshire marble. This is black in colour and can take a high polish, being formerly worked at Ashford-in-the-Water near Bakewell.

Quarrying is important to the inhabitants of the Peak District as a source of employment and valuable to the nation as a source of economic wealth but quarries can often be a serious disfigurement of the landscape, particularly where the installation of modern plant has led to quarries of gigantic size and with machinery which represents a large factory in itself. Crushing plants installed at some quarries can cover the surrounding area with a white coating of limestone dust, which in extreme cases can stifle vegetation and is always unsightly. Where lime burning takes place a pall of black smoke can hang over the countryside, although the use of oil for fuel is reducing this nuisance.

The effect of all this upon a landscape which is of such great value as a lung for large urban populations can be serious. Near Buxton the number of great quarries led the planners of the national park boundary to exclude them by drawing a great enclave into the park, and it can be argued that quarrying defaces a few well defined areas leaving the majority of the Peak undefiled. The Planning Board takes the view that the existing quarries must be accepted but that areas free from quarrying must be sacrosanct; all proposals for new mineral workings in the national park are very carefully scrutinised and the promoter must put up a very strong case to secure permission for even the most inconspicuous quarry.

COAL MINING

There are parts of three coalfields in Derbyshire. The main one is in the east, extending from the Yorkshire border southwards to Stanton to the east of Derby. This coalfield extends eastwards into Nottinghamshire, where the same seams are worked, although they are progressively deeper as they go east. There is a small area of coal mining in the extreme south of Derbyshire around Swadlincote and there was formerly coal mining in the north-west in the Whaley Bridge and New Mills areas.

The industry is an ancient one and the earliest references to coal mining go back to the thirteenth century. This must refer to what is now known as opencast mining but there are records of bell-pit working in the fourteenth century.

Until the improvement of transport during the nineteenth century the Derbyshire coal industry was hampered by the high cost of conveying the coal to the markets as the only reasonably cheap means was by water and the county is not well endowed with navigable rivers. Nevertheless fortunes were made by families in the mine-owning business.

The development of the railways enabled Derbyshire coal to compete on equal terms with that from north-east England and a great expansion followed. Today many of the older collieries have closed or are on the point of closing. The abandoned colliery surface plant is being cleared and the spoil tips are being reshaped and planted with grass and trees, bringing dramatic improvement to the landscape. The main areas of coal production are moving east to the deeper seams beneath Nottinghamshire and these same seams beneath Leicestershire and Lincolnshire are where the future of this vital industry will doubtless be found.

Hazlebadge Hall, south of Bradwell. In the gable are the arms of the Vernon and Swynnerton families and the date 1549.

Holme Bridge, Bakewell. A packhorse bridge of 1664 across the river Wye to the north of the town.

Towns and villages

ALFRETON

Early closing Wednesday; market day Friday.

A town of the coalfield, Alfreton is of ancient origin. The main street becomes wide as it runs uphill, with a few pleasant old buildings. Before coal mining became the staple industry the making of brown earthenware and stockings were the main trades. There is a church of the late Norman period, although much altered subsequently.

ASHBOURNE

Early closing Wednesday; market day Saturday.

The sloping Market Place has many interesting nooks and crannies. There are several impressive streets lined with houses of the eighteenth and early nineteenth centuries, when Ashbourne must have been very prosperous. The best is Church Street, with the old Grammar School of 1585. Opposite is the Mansion House, early eighteenth-century, where lived Dr Taylor, who was often visited by his friend Samuel Johnson.

A feature of Ashbourne is the number of almshouses to be seen in groups around the town, a sign of the benevolence of former townsmen.

On Shrove Tuesday and Ash Wednesday football is played with much gusto. Play commences by the Henmore Brook and usually continues in the brook itself although the shopkeepers wisely board up their windows. The teams are the 'Upards' and the 'Downards', those born above or below the bridge, but this is not the sort of game in which undue emphasis is placed upon rules.

ASHFORD-IN-THE-WATER

This is an attractive village, as pleasant as its name. The nineteenth-century church retains the tympanum of the Norman building over the south door, showing a wild boar and wolf under the Tree of Life. There are several large houses, such as Ashford Hall of 1785. The water of the name is the river Wye and there are three old bridges, the Sheepwash Bridge being especially attractive in its lush, well wooded setting.

ASHOVER

Set in the Amber Valley among fine moorlands, Ashover has a pleasant centre with the Crispin Inn close to the church. The inn, if the rather wordy sign above the door is to be believed, dates from 1416, when men returned from the battle of Agincourt, fought on St Crispin's Day. Lead mining was once important here and in the church is a lead font of about 1200.

BAKEWELL
Early closing Thursday; market day Monday.

Bakewell has Saxon origins; there is a Saxon cross in the churchyard and there are traces of Saxon earthworks on Castle Hill to the west of the town (chapter 5). The fine church (see chapter 6) is well sited part way up the hill among a maze of narrow lanes overlooking the town centre on the plain of the river Wye.

The centre of Bakewell is the square, presided over by the Rutland Arms hotel of 1804. To one side Bath Gardens serve as a reminder of an abortive attempt to develop the town as a spa town and in Bridge Street, leading to the river, is the Market Hall of the late seventeenth century. In King Street, leading up the hill to the church is the former Town Hall of 1709 (but it looks much older).

There are a number of fine houses in Bakewell including Bagshaw Hall on the hillside, Catcliffe House in King Street, and, across the Town Bridge of 1300, the eighteenth-century Castle Hill. Across the old packhorse bridge, a little higher up the river, is Holme Hall of 1626.

Bakewell has an important cattle market and on Mondays is a place of much bustle and business. There are pleasant walks to be had in the meadows by the river as well as into the surrounding country. Most of the buildings are small in scale and much of Bakewell has the character of a village. Well kept and orderly as a consequence of centuries of control by two ducal estates, it is nevertheless very much a town with a good range of shops and is the centre of life in its own area.

BAMFORD
A large village in the Derwent Valley close to its junction with the Hope Valley, Bamford was greatly developed towards the end of the nineteenth century as a place of residence for people who travelled to Sheffield by train to work. The church, which dates from 1861, is by Butterfield.

BARLBOROUGH
Barlborough Hall dates from 1583 and was probably designed by Robert Smythson. Square in plan, with corner turrets, it is a smaller member of the group of Elizabethan houses that includes Hardwick Hall. Now a school, it is occasionally open to the public. The hall is approached along a lime avenue from the village, with its much restored church and several attractive old buildings.

BASLOW
Situated at the northern end of Chatsworth Park, this large village has developed a good deal in modern times. At the heart is still the pleasant old church and the ancient bridge across the Derwent with a tiny toll house at one end, the doorway of which is only 3½ feet (1.1 m) high.

Little John's grave at Hathersage.

BEELEY

Beeley is one of the Chatsworth estate villages, with a good deal of fanciful architecture of the 1840s. 2 miles (3 km) north-east is Hob Hurst's House, a barrow of the bronze age (1600-1000 BC).

BELPER

Early closing Wednesday; market day Saturday.

Although there was once a hunting lodge of 'Beau Repaire' here (hence the name), the town as we see it now is virtually the creation of the Strutt family, who from 1771 developed the textile industry here, using the water power of the river Derwent. Some of the vast mills on the north side of the town have unfortunately been demolished but enough remains to indicate the once flourishing condition of the place. There are still streets of workers' housing to be seen and among the houses is the Unitarian chapel of 1788 with a monument to Jedediah Strutt.

BIRCHOVER

Birchover is a small village between Winster and Youlgreave. One of the few working gritstone quarries can be seen here close to the road and nearby, on Stanton Moor (owned by the National Trust), are several abandoned ones. There too are several barrows of the bronze age and the Nine Ladies (see chapter 5) and Doll Tor stone circles. A tower can be seen which was built to celebrate the passing of the Reform Bill in 1832.

There are a number of gritstone crags around the village and behind the Druid's Arms Inn are the Druid Stones, including two 'rocking stones'.

BOLSOVER

Early closing Wednesday; market day Friday.

Bolsover began as a dependency of its castle, both probably dating from the eleventh century. The town was laid out as a grid of streets aligned along the edge of the limestone cliff, with the castle at one end and the church at the other. The market place was originally rectangular but has become triangular owing to later encroachments.

Below the ridge from which the castle (see chapter 7) dominates the valley there is a vast expanse of industry, colliery plant and the like, but also New Bolsover, a model village built by the colliery company in 1888 with terraced houses around three sides of a green.

BUXTON

Early closing Wednesday; market day Saturday.

Buxton waters were known to the Romans for their curative properties but the development of the town owes most to successive Dukes of Devonshire. The outstanding architectural feature of the town is the Crescent, designed by John Carr of York and completed in 1784. This contained two hotels, shops and the assembly room at the eastern end. St Ann's Hotel is still there but the rest of the building is now the public library of the town with the splendid assembly room as the reference library. This is open to the public during library hours. Higher up the slope, the Great Stables were built around a great circular courtyard, later roofed over with a vast dome when the building was converted to a hospital in 1859.

The area around the Crescent was laid out to plans by John White and his son during the early nineteenth century and they also designed the block of buildings known as The Square, just west of the Crescent, and St John's church to the north-west. Immediately to the south of the Crescent are the Slopes, terraced walks on the steep hillside laid out by Sir Jeffrey Wyattville in 1818. These were originally enclosed by a wall and iron gates.

These Georgian developments were supplemented by a wave of Victorian expansion following the arrival of the railways in the 1860s. To the west of the Crescent, the Pavilion Gardens were laid out by Edward Milner for a private company, with an iron and glass pavilion along the north side. In 1875 this was enlarged by a large octagonal concert hall, also in iron and glass, and a theatre behind the pavilion. In 1903 a further theatre was added, the Opera House, designed by Frank Matcham, the prolific London theatre architect. The gardens were extended in 1880 and the Serpentine Walks added further west.

Within the town one is scarcely aware of the many quarries close at hand for Buxton is set in a great saucer of hills. Many of the streets are lined with trees and Spring Gardens still retains some of those glazed roofs across the pavement which the Victorians considered essential to a holiday resort.

Today Buxton is a popular centre for visitors to the surrounding country and, after some years of neglect, the distinctive buildings and gardens of the town are being reburbished. The Opera House, which in spite of its name was rarely used for opera, has been restored and is now the setting for the opera productions of the Buxton Festival held in late July and early August each year.

CASTLETON

Magnificently sited below Peveril Castle (see chapter 5) the village began as a planned medieval borough to serve the needs of the castle. The street plan forms a square, once the market place, although later building has encroached on the space. On the north side is the church, largely rebuilt in 1837 but retaining

The Pavilion Gardens, Buxton. Part of the Conservatory and a turret of the Opera House on the left and The Square on the right.

earlier work. Along the east and south sides traces of the medieval ditch can still be seen. Castleton has many attractive old buildings, among the best being Castleton Hall, now the youth hostel. For the Garland Day custom on 29th May, see chapter 4.

CHAPEL-EN-LE-FRITH
Early closing Wednesday; market day Thursday.

Chapel-en-le-Frith lies just outside the national park, to the north of Buxton. The curious name is derived from the chapel built in 1225 by the keepers of the Forest (or frith) of the Peak. This structure was replaced by the present church in the fourteenth century. In 1733 the tower and south facade were converted to a classical style.

Formerly the town was little more than a single long street with innumerable inns to cater for the needs of weary travellers crossing the dreary wastes of the Peak.

CHELMORTON

This is a village of the limestone plateau south-east of Buxton. The old church with its sturdy tower and spire looks out across a pattern of long narrow fields divided by stone walls, indicating the enclosure of the cultivation strips of the medieval open fields. The larger, square fields are later enclosures.

CHESTERFIELD
Early closing Wednesday; market days Monday, Friday and Saturday.

Chesterfield is the second largest town in Derbyshire, with a population of about seventy thousand, and is the centre of the coal-mining area. There was a fort here in Roman times, roughly where the parish church now stands, but it became a purely civil settlement about AD 130. The town gives little indication today of such ancient origins but there are more traces of its past to be seen than the superficial observer might suppose.

The centre of the town is the market place and this area has been transformed and greatly improved in recent years; indeed numerous awards have been bestowed on the operation. On Low Pavement is the old Peacock Inn, a timber-framed building of about 1500 now adapted as the tourist information office on the ground floor, with the large room above used for temporary displays. There are a number of other old buildings in this area, often skilfully incorporated into new groups of buildings.

To the west of the market place area stands the Town Hall, a typical municipal building of the 1930s, impressively sited at the top of the slope leading down to West Bars. This area is on a much bigger scale than the older parts of the town and the contrast is not unpleasant. Below the Town Hall are gardens with the modern court house on one side and at the foot of the hill the more sober buildings of the post office finance department. Southwards again, across the town centre relief road is Queen's Park.

A new road now carries through traffic around the town centre and it is possible once more to appreciate in peace the church (see chapter 6) set in an attractive churchyard.

Chelmorton. Close to the village (running diagonally across the picture) are the narrow fields of ancient enclosure. In the foreground and distance are rectangular fields dating from the 1809 Enclosure Act.

About 1 mile (1.6 km) north-east of the town centre is Tapton House, built about 1800, which was the last home of George Stephenson, the great engineer. The building is now a school. Stephenson lies buried in Holy Trinity church, Newbold Road, where there is a stained glass window to his memory.

The Revolution House is described in chapter 8.

CLAY CROSS
Early closing Wednesday; market day Saturday.

This small industrial town, developed by the Clay Cross Company, was founded by George Stephenson in 1837. He is said to have found coal whilst building the Clay Cross Tunnel for the North Midland Railway and capitalised on his find by building the town to mine the coal. The main industries are now engineering and the ironworks. The large church of St Bartholomew of 1851 is by Alfred Stevens with glass by Morris and Burne-Jones.

CLOWNE
Early closing Wednesday; market day Friday.

Clowne is a colliery village surrounded by attractive country on the Nottinghamshire border. The old village lies to the south, where the church has Norman work, a fifteenth-century tower and in the chancel the tomb of William Inskip, who died in 1582 having held the benefice for fifty-four years right through the Reformation, like the better known Vicar of Bray.

CRESWELL
The model colliery village was laid out by Percy Houfton for the colliery company between 1896 and 1900 at the same time as the sinking of the pit. The church was begun in 1899 and the whole forms an interesting example of enlightened industrial development for the times. For the famous Creswell Crags, see chapter 5.

CRICH
It is rare for English villages to stand on hilltops, even in Derbyshire, but Crich (pronounced 'Crych') is that rarity. There are distant views in all directions, especially from Crich Stand, which was built as a war memorial for the Sherwood Foresters, the regiment of Derbyshire and Nottinghamshire. The beacon is lit each night and there is public access to the top of the tower.

The church is a notable one with fine Norman and fourteenth-century work. Crich was once a prosperous lead-mining centre and the market cross still stands amid the rather higgledy-piggledy jumble of streets. For the National Tramway Museum see chapter 8.

CROMFORD
Cromford was virtually the creation of Sir Richard Arkwright. In 1771 he established the first successful cotton-spinning mill here. When he arrived the place was no more than a scattered hamlet relying on lead mining and a little farming. All this changed with the building of the mill and a new settlement for the workers had to be created.

The centre of the village is the Market Place, presided over by the Greyhound Inn built by Arkwright in 1778. The main road,

44

A6, was built as a turnpike road between 1816 and 1818 to improve what had previously been very poor access. Beyond this road Mill Lane leads to the forbidding, gaunt mill buildings (see chapter 9). By going a little further one comes to the wharf of the Cromford Canal (see chapter 9) and to the bridge across the Derwent, which dates back to the fifteenth century. By the bridge is a little fishing pavilion of the early eighteenth century and the church built by Arkwright in 1792. Close by are the gates to Willersley Castle built by Arkwright for himself in 1789-90 and now a residential centre.

The village built to house the workers is found by walking in the opposite direction from the Market Place, up the hill signposted to Wirksworth. The stone terraces on the left of this road are among those built by Arkwright but perhaps the best place to see what an early industrial revolution housing scheme was like is North Street, a cul-de-sac of stone terraces, three storeys high, with the school at the end of the street.

Cromford has come down to us as a well preserved example of one of the first factory villages because Arkwright's son reduced the scale of operations and, although he kept the business going, he undertook no further developments. Until the Arkwrights sold the business in 1926 very little changed in either village or mills.

For the restored railway workshops at High Peak Junction, see chapter 9.

DALE ABBEY

The tiny village of Dale Abbey is remarkably rural and secluded, considering that Derby and Nottingham are each 8 miles (13 km) away in opposite directions. The Abbey is said to have originated in a hermit's cell founded by a Derby baker who was told to come here in a vision. The cave is still to be seen, enlarged in the eighteenth century and fitted with windows. The abbey was founded about 1200.

The only remaining fragment is the arch of the east window of the chancel, which stands over 17 feet (5.2 m) high, all the more poignant for standing by a farmyard quite unspoiled by mown grass or notice boards. Perhaps even more remarkable is the church of Dale Abbey, one of the oddest in Britain. Only 25 by 26 feet (7.6 by 7.9 m), it is under the same roof as a private house, once the Bluebell Inn. Inside the church are box pews, gallery and pulpit as well as some late thirteenth-century wall paintings.

DARLEY DALE

This is the name given to the broad valley of the Derwent to the north of Matlock, now scattered with suburban development.

Close to the river is the old village centre with the medieval church of St Helen. There is a fine stained glass window of about 1860 by William Morris in the south transept, in reaction to the over-florid style of the time. In the churchyard is a famous yew tree reputed to be over two thousand years old. Even if this claim is not believed, the tree is certainly among the largest yews. Derwent Bridge is fifteenth-century.

On the eastern side of the main A6 road is Stancliffe Hall, the home of Sir Joseph Whitworth (1803-87), pioneer of machine tools and armament manufacture. His name is immortalised in the standard screw thread as well as in the Whitworth Institute, which stands on the main road in a small park, the incomplete first phase of what he intended as a philanthropic new town. Higher up the hillside are extensive nurseries as the soil is especially suited to the cultivation of heathers.

DERBY

Early closing Wednesday; market days Friday and Saturday.

Derby can claim to be the newest city in Britain for the borough was raised to that

The last fragment of Dale Abbey, the arch of the east window. The house, of Premonstratensian Canons, was founded about 1200.

St Mary's Bridge, Derby, rebuilt between 1788 and 1793 by Thomas Harrison.

dignity only in 1977. But Derby is an ancient place. There was a Roman fort here by about AD 48 at a site on Belper Road now known as Strutts Park. This seems to have been abandoned and replaced by another about AD 78-81 on the side of the Derwent at Little Chester. This fort was occupied into the fifth century and gave rise to a thriving civil settlement of the name *Derventio*. The settlement survived into the Anglo-Saxon period but whether there was continuous occupation into later times is not yet established.

Doubts about the continuity of habitation are the greater because the Anglian settlement of Northworthy occupied a different site somewhat to the south, where the Markeaton Brook joins the Derwent. It was this settlement which was taken over by the Danes, who called it *Deoraby* (hence Derby), and it became one of the five boroughs of the Danelaw which controlled the East Midlands.

Medieval Derby was largely a one-street town with five of its six churches strung out along the street now represented by Queen Street, Irongate, Corn Market and St Peter's Street, and this is still the backbone of the modern city. The town remained a modest place until the eighteenth century, a long straggling town on the west side of the Derwent with a single bridge across the river, St Mary's Bridge. Daniel Defoe described Derby as 'a town of gentry rather than trade' early in the eighteenth century. Already, however, things were changing and close to the bridge the first factory in the modern sense had already been built and the Silk Mill, still

there and now used as the Industrial Museum (see chapter 8), was a portent of things to come. The later eighteenth century became a time of great change with more mills being built, the start of porcelain manufacture, and with inhabitants as innovative as Erasmus Darwin, physician, freethinker, radical and poet, Joseph Wright, painter, and many more.

The sale of Nun's Green, the only open space in the town, by the town council resulted in the building of the fine Georgian houses in Friar Gate, architecturally much the best street in the city. The loss of Nun's Green resulted in a sense of grievance on the part of the townspeople, only assuaged in 1840 when Joseph Strutt gave to the town the Arboretum, the first public park in Britain specifically laid out as such.

Development in the nineteenth century was rapid, but expansion was restricted by a ring of large gardens and small parks attached to the houses of the still numerous gentry. Eventually pressure of population, as well as industrial pollution, drove the gentry out and the arrival of the railways in 1839 was to transform Derby. In 1844 three competing companies combined to form the Midland Railway, with headquarters in Derby. During the nineteenth century the population increased tenfold but the twentieth century has seen developments no less dramatic. In 1908 Rolls-Royce began manufacturing motor cars and later started production of the engines for aircraft that now monopolise their vast works, and the more traditional textile industries were growing apace with the development of the great

46

Courtauld works following the First World War.

The centre of the city has subsequently undergone great changes. The Market Place is still the centre of town, presided over by the Guildhall, but the northern side of the square is dominated by the Assembly Rooms. This building contains the principal assembly hall of the city and was built in 1971-76 to replace the old Assembly Rooms destroyed by fire in 1963. The new building is much bigger than its predecessor. Most of the streets leading off the Market Place are pleasant shopping streets, some reserved for pedestrian use. Southwards from the Market Place is a large area of enclosed shopping malls, well knitted into the older fabric of the city. The Playhouse Theatre is in this area.

Leading northwards from the Market Place is Irongate, which provides a fine view of the splendid cathedral tower. Opposite the cathedral (see chapter 6) is St Mary's Gate, the street which still gives an impression of the county town of gentry which Derby once was. At the far end of the street is the County Hall, built about 1660, now housing the Crown Courts, and close by are the buildings which were the county offices until the county council moved to Matlock in 1955. Round the corner, in Bold Lane, the building now used as magistrate's courts was once the theatre, and before that a malthouse. Close by, in The Wardwick, is the Public Library and Museum and Art Gallery (see chapter 8), St Werburgh's church, where Dr Samuel Johnson was married, and several fine old houses, of which that known as the Jacobean House is perhaps the best.

There is much of interest to the visitor in Derby but it will take a little trouble to find it. However, the city council has placed display boards at suitable points giving an account of the history of the surrounding area, often with illustrations of buildings now gone. But the city is in no sense a tourist town, and southwards from the city centre is a great area dominated by industry, where Rolls-Royce and the British Rail Technical Centre are among the mainstays of the local economy.

DOVEDALE

Dovedale has been celebrated since the romantic taste for 'savage' scenery developed during the eighteenth century and has never been more admired than today. On summer weekends the number of visitors can be so great as almost to banish any thoughts of savage grandeur but in winter, and in mid-week even in summer, one can enjoy the dale as it should be seen. In the right conditions the walk from the car park at the southern end through Dovedale, Milldale, Wolfscote Dale and Beresford Dale is unrivalled in Britain.

DRONFIELD

Formerly a prosperous market town, Dronfield still has a number of fine buildings from previous centuries, although it has suffered by being divided by the railway, which was built in the valley floor. Formerly the heavy traffic of the main Chesterfield to Sheffield road added to the divisive effect but this now uses the bypass to the west. The church with its fine spire presides over the town centre and the Manor House, now the public library, is of the early eighteenth century.

DUFFIELD

Duffield grew up around a great castle, one of the largest in England. Very little remains above ground and the site is a public open space. Town Street has many good houses of the eighteenth century and there are more in Tamworth Street. Duffield Hall is Jacobean in origin but was transformed in 1871. It is now offices. Among the delights of Duffield is the Baptist chapel of 1830, with attendant house, almshouses and graveyard. The church is near the river, isolated from the town, mainly fourteenth-century but restored in 1846 and again in 1896.

EDALE

Edale is a broad valley on the southern flanks of Kinder Scout with a number of hamlets known as Booths; hence Barber Booth, Upper Booth, Ollerbrook Booth. Grindsbrook Booth developed as the centre of the valley community in the nineteenth century when a railway station was built there and is now often regarded as the village of Edale. It is a popular base for walking on Kinder Scout and the southern terminus of the Pennine Way. There is a national park information centre at Fieldhead.

ETWALL

This is an attractive village with a church of many periods, somewhat heavily restored. Of the eighteenth-century hall only the gates survive, made by Robert Bakewell about 1730, and now to be seen at the secondary school, which occupies the site of the hall. Etwall Hospital was founded as almshouses by Sir John Port in 1550. The present buildings date from 1681 and are in brick around three sides of a court. The residents of the hospital have the north aisle of the church as their chapel, which is equipped with stalls for the purpose.

EYAM

A village noted as the plague village for the visitation of the plague in 1665 and commemorated on Plague Sunday each year (see chapter 4). In the main street near the church are the Plague Cottages and the graves of some of those who died then can still be seen. The

The sundial on the wall of Eyam church.

church was much restored in the nineteenth century but there is a Norman font and in the churchyard a fine Saxon cross that has retained its head and arms over the centuries. A Barmote still meets here occasionally to deal with disputes in lead mining (see chapter 10) and mining still takes place in the vicinity, although usually for the associated minerals rather than for lead ore itself.

GLOSSOP
Early closing Tuesday; market days Friday and Saturday.

The town was formerly much dependent upon the cotton industry. Old Glossop is the original nucleus, still with its church and old houses. The modern town began when the Dukes of Norfolk were the landowners and it used to be known as Howards Town. The centre is Norfolk Square with the Town Hall of 1838 a dignified centrepiece.

GREAT LONGSTONE
A village to the north of Bakewell, Great Longstone has a single street and an ancient church. The hall of 1747 is one of the few brick buildings in the Peak, very plain and seen from the street down an avenue of elms. **Little Longstone** has some old houses. In front of one of them the stocks are still to be seen. Close by is Monsal Head, a well known viewpoint from which Monsal Dale and Millers Dale can be seen in panorama.

HARTINGTON
Hartington is a large village close to the upper course of the river Dove. The ancient church presides over the place, across the valley from Hartington Hall of 1611, now a youth hostel. The Market Place has some old houses and the 'Town Hall' (built as a shop) of 1836. The Charles Cotton Hotel commemorates the author of the second part of *The Compleat Angler*. Nearby, in Beresford Dale, is the fishing pavilion he built in 1674 and which can be seen from the footpath although it is on private land.

HATHERSAGE
This is a large village in the Derwent valley. The original nucleus was high up around the church, later extending downhill in a single main street, but there is much modern development. The church has brasses of the Eyre family and in the churchyard the reputed grave of Robin Hood's companion Little John. Charlotte Bronte stayed here and described the place in *Jane Eyre* under the name of Morton.

HAYFIELD
Early closing Wednesday; market day Monday.

Hayfield is an industrial village to the west of Kinder Scout, which may be conveniently approached from here. There are cotton and paper mills and a church of 1818 with very thin cast iron columns and the original box pews.

HEAGE
This large village has a curious church. The medieval building was much damaged in a storm in 1545, rebuilt in 1646-61 and then had a cross wing added in 1826 to make a T-shaped building. The Morley Park ironworks to the south-west were started in the late eighteenth century and remains of two of the blast furnaces survive as flat-topped pyramids. Heage windmill is a mid nineteenth-century tower mill with an ogee cap and six sails.

HEANOR
Early closing Wednesday; market day Saturday.

An industrial town, Heanor formerly had several collieries. These are now closed and much work has been done to restore land devastated by spoil heaps. The church has a fine Perpendicular west tower, the remainder being of 1868. Inside is a memorial to Samuel Watson of 1715. He did much of the carving at Chatsworth, and his work was of such a quality that it has been confused with that of Grinling Gibbons.

HOPE
A large village on the main road through the broad valley to which it gives its name. The church has fourteenth-century work, although much rebuilt and modified. Among the monuments are two thirteenth-century slabs to

officials of the Peak Forest and in the churchyard is a Saxon cross shaft. There are many attractive old houses, especially along the minor road leading to Edale. A little south of the village and quite distinct from it are the large cement works which, though the subject of much controversy and dominating this part of the valley, do provide valuable employment in an area without much other industry.

HOPTON

Hopton Hall has been the home of the Gell family since the fourteenth century; the present building is Elizabethan but was altered in the eighteenth century. The crinkle-crankle or serpentine wall to the garden and a tower-like summerhouse can be seen from the road. On the Wirksworth road can be seen the Sir Philip Gell Almshouses of 1719-22. To the north-east of the village are the quarries which produced the famous Hopton Wood stone.

ILKESTON

Early closing Wednesday; market day Saturday.

A busy industrial town, formerly with collieries, Ilkeston has ancient origins. There are few reminders of these to be seen now but the church of St Mary, although heavily restored, has a remarkable survival in the early fourteenth-century stone chancel screen. The church was enlarged in 1910 by moving the tower stone by stone to allow the nave to be doubled in length. The hilltop situation of the town provides many extensive views and although the place is not well endowed with interesting buildings the Bennerley Viaduct of 1867 is 500 feet (150 m) long as it crosses the Erwash Valley to the north-east.

LONG EATON

Early closing Thursday; market days Friday and Saturday.

Like many Derbyshire towns, Long Eaton has ancient origins but began to develop early in the nineteenth century with the rise of the lacemaking industry. There are extensive factories still engaged in the lace industry but many other industries have been more recently established here. The town centre is pleasantly open in aspect, with many trees. In 1868 the old church behind the market place was incorporated as the south aisle in a new church by G. E. Street. Trent College on Derby Road is a well known public school. The grounds contain an excellent collection of rare trees.

MATLOCK

Early closing Thursday; market days Tuesday and Friday.

The town has developed from a number of hamlets, hence there are several Matlocks. The principal one is Matlock Town, by the river with a widened fifteenth-century bridge. Above, Matlock Bank is the area of the hydros, a phase of the holiday industry now passed. The original and largest hydro, Smedleys, is now the Derbyshire County Offices.

Matlock Bath lies lower down the river Derwent as it cuts through a great gorge in the limestone with the great cliff of High Tor on one side. A number of tepid springs were the cause of the development of the place early in the eighteenth century as a very rustic and secluded watering place. Byron and Ruskin both came here, it being one of the recognised places for the romantic contemplation of scenery. It retains much of its beauty, if not its seclusion, with the houses climbing the steep hillsides above the river. To see Matlock Bath to advantage one must leave the main valley road and climb up one of the lanes threading the hillside.

MELBOURNE

Melbourne is a small town that seems to have moved its centre over the centuries. The church and hall now stand well to the east of

Cable cars take visitors to the Heights of Abraham at Matlock Bath.

The chapel of the Moravian Settlement at Ockbrook, founded in 1750.

the market place and there was once a large castle close by. This was built in the fourteenth century but was allowed to decay slowly so that today very little is to be seen above ground. A reminder is to be found in the name of Castle Street, and Castle Mills now cover much of the site.

Today the town is an attractive place with its large church (see chapter 6) and hall (see chapter 7). In High Street is a cruck building and in Chapel Street is the Baptist chapel of 1750. The town is the centre of a market gardening district and the intensively cultivated fields make a strange landscape.

The city of Melbourne in Australia was named after the second Lord Melbourne, British Prime Minister at the time of its founding. His title was derived from the Derbyshire town, which thus has links at one remove with its great Australian namesake.

MILFORD

Milford was a mill town, as its name indicates, founded by Jedediah Strutt, who built his first mill here in 1780, using the water power of the river Derwent. There was once a series of early mill buildings along both sides of the river but almost all were demolished in the 1950s and 1960s. The weirs used to control the river and the bridge built in 1792 to carry the main road across the river are still to be seen. Some of the stone terraces of millworkers' houses still stand on the hillside.

MONYASH

Sited high on the limestone to the west of Bakewell, this is a village formerly of much importance for it was once a market town and lead-mining centre. There is still a fine, ancient church.

NEW MILLS

A small industrial town at the confluence of the rivers Sett and Goyt, New Mills developed from a series of hamlets, with the mills of the place-name using the power of the Sett as it rushes down from Kinder Scout. The river here has carved a spectacular gorge in the massive gritstone, known as the Torrs, which can be seen over the parapet of the bridge in Union Road, and explored on foot by taking the industrial history trail which starts near the corner of Rock Mill Lane and Union Road. Close by is the Heritage Centre, telephone: New Mills (0663) 46904.

Cotton finishing, especially calico printing, became the main local industry and the visitor will soon be aware of his proximity to Manchester in this part of Derbyshire. A number of eighteenth-century buildings remain and the High Street still gives a typical early mill town appearance.

OCKBROOK

The Moravian Settlement was founded here in 1750 and the chapel and terraced houses make a distinctive part of the village. Only the tower and spire of the medieval church remain, the rest being nineteenth-century. A sixteenth-century screen was brought here from Wigston's Hospital, Leicester.

RENISHAW

The Sitwells built Renishaw Hall in 1625 and shortly afterwards set up the ironworks, becoming, for a time, the biggest makers of nails in the world. Coal mines were added to their formidable industrial enterprise. The wealth thus created was used to enlarge the hall and, at the close of the nineteenth century, to lay out the spectacular formal gardens. This work was done by Sir George Sitwell, famous through the autobiography of his son, Sir Osbert Sitwell. Indeed, to readers of the numerous works of Sir George's three children, Edith, Osbert and Sacheverell, Renishaw will be familiar territory even though they may never have set foot here. The hall is not open to the public, although frequently open to organised groups, and is still owned by the Sitwells.

REPTON

This quiet village was once a place of great importance for a monastery founded here in the seventh century became one of the principal residences of the kings of Mercia. The monastery was destroyed by the Vikings during the winter of 874-5 but a new foundation, an Augustinian Priory, was completed in 1172 and this lasted until the Dissolution of 1538. The buildings of the priory passed into private hands until 1557, when Sir John Port founded a school in part of the old buildings. It is this foundation that has grown into the famous public school, which has expanded into a number of other buildings about the village.

The cross still marks the centre of the place and from here there is a good view of the fascinating church (see chapter 6), with the old Priory Arch to the right giving entry to the main school buildings. In the opposite direction the long High Street is lined with pleasant buildings of many dates but all combining in a most attractive series of street scenes.

RIPLEY

Early closing Wednesday; market day Saturday.

Near this hilltop industrial town, Butterley Hall was the eighteenth-century home of Benjamin Outram, one of the founders of the Butterley Company, pioneers of the industrial revolution. It is now the county police headquarters. For the Midland Railway Centre see chapter 9.

The Cross at Repton, with the spire of St Wystan's church in the background.

Swarkestone. The summer house of the long-vanished home of the Harpur family, seen from the gate that leads into a field — once a walled garden.

SHARDLOW

The old village was centred on the crossroads where the Dog and Duck public house now stands. Close by are the hall, built in the seventeenth and eighteenth centuries and now converted into offices, and the church of the nineteenth century.

To the south of the old village is the canal port developed with the building of the Trent and Mersey Canal by James Brindley in 1777. Here was the place where goods carried by barges up the Trent were transhipped to narrow boats for the journey into the Midlands. Inlets were constructed off the canal and a whole canal community developed with workshops for such crafts as smithing, rope-making and boatbuilding as well as warehouses, cottages and the essential public houses. Trade declined with the coming of the railways in the 1840s but has revived in recent years and Shardlow today is a busy place with many pleasure craft.

STAVELEY

Early closing Wednesday; market day Friday.

Although now dominated by the vast iron-works and other industries, Staveley was once a feudal village owned by the Frechville family and their hall still stands just north of the church. The latter is mainly thirteenth-century and the Frechville Chapel contains stained glass of 1676 and monuments to the family. There are other old buildings but they are not easy to find amid the modern developments.

STONEY MIDDLETON

Just off the Derwent Valley in Middleton Dale, with its houses in clusters on the steep sides of the narrow valley, Stoney Middleton was once a lead-mining village and is now a centre of limestone quarrying. In 1759 the very odd octagonal church was added to the medieval tower with a result which is curious rather than beautiful. Some of the old houses in the village display architectural oddities in their details.

SWADLINCOTE

Early closing Wednesday; market day Saturday.

Swadlincote is an industrial town with large pits where clay has been quarried for the making of pottery of all kinds. The town is the centre of the south Derbyshire coalfield.

THORPE

Close to the southern entrance to Dovedale, Thorpe has a Norman church. Thorpe Pastures is a great expanse of common land including Thorpe Cloud, a conical hill from which fine views may be had.

TIDESWELL

Tideswell is a small town nestling in a valley amid the limestone uplands. The buildings are strung out along the valley sides, enclosing several small squares, once no doubt market places, for Tideswell was a prosperous commercial centre in former times.

TISSINGTON

An estate village of the Fitzherbert family in the south of the National Park, Tissington is approached from the main Ashbourne to Buxton road between gate piers and along a stately avenue of trees. Very neat and tidy, the hall faces the church across the triangular green with the houses grouped around and ducks on the village pond. A well-dressing ceremony is held on Ascension Day.

WHALEY BRIDGE

Early closing Wednesday; market day Friday.

A small town, formerly much engaged in the cotton-finishing trades, Whaley Bridge lies in the Goyt Valley just beyond the western borders of the national park. The place became important as one of the terminal points of the Peak Forest Canal when it was built in 1800. Here goods from the Lancashire mills were taken from the narrow boats and hauled up a steep incline railway, worked by a stationary engine; from the top they were carried along the High Peak Tramway across the Peak to Cromford, where a further canal led to the waterways of the Midlands. The canal and canal basin are still in use for pleasure traffic and the site of the incline can be clearly seen. There are pleasant walks along the towpath and just to the west of the town is one of the two reservoirs which serve the canal. Houses are set among trees overlooking the water and the sails of small craft add to the interest of the scene.

WINSTER

Once a centre of lead mining, Winster is still a large village with many fine houses of the seventeenth and eighteenth centuries. In the wide main street is the Market Hall with an upper storey supported by arches, now filled in. The nineteenth-century church has a curious interior with columns down the middle of the nave.

WIRKSWORTH

Early closing Wednesday; market day Tuesday.

The old centre of the lead mining industry,

Wirksworth lies just outside the south-eastern boundary of the national park. At the Moot Hall the Barmote Court still meets. The hilly site has resulted in the main streets having a picturesque jumbled appearance as they lead to the Market Place, and they are lined with many old houses.

Wirksworth has been the subject of a remarkable project to enhance and reinvigorate the town. This was initiated by the Civic Trust in 1979 and is being continued by a local organisation. Buildings have been repaired streets and the Market Place repaved, trees planted and, perhaps more important than all this, a new sense of well-being developed which has led to new businesses being opened. There is a Heritage Centre and the National Stone Centre is being developed just to the north of the town. To appreciate fully the transformation, one needs to be able to remember the rundown condition of the town in the mid 1970s but some idea of the sense of revival will be apparent to any visitor. Several awards have already been conferred on the town for a project which was always intended to show how a small, neglected town could be revived, largely by its own efforts.

Winster Market Hall.

53

Darley Dale, the church of St Helen. On the left is part of the enormous yew tree, among the largest, and probably the oldest, in Britain.

12
Tourist information centres

Ashbourne: 13 Market Place, Ashbourne DE6 1EU. Telephone: Ashbourne (0335) 43666.
Bakewell: Old Market Hall, Bridge Street, Bakewell DE4 1DS. Telephone: Bakewell (0639) 813227.
Buxton: The Crescent, Buxton SK17 6BQ. Telephone: Buxton (0298) 25106.
Chesterfield: The Peacock Information and Heritage Centre, Low Pavement, Chesterfield S40 1PB. Telephone: Chesterfield (0246) 207777.
Derby: Central Library, The Wardwick, Derby DE1 4HS. Telephone: Derby (0332) 290664.
Glossop: Station Forecourt, Norfolk Street, Glossop SK13 8BF. Telephone: Glossop (04574) 5920.
Matlock Bath: The Pavilion, Matlock Bath DE4 3NR. Telephone: Matlock (0629) 55082.

The information centre at Bakewell is also a Peak National Park information centre. There are other National Park information centres at Castleton and Edale (see chapter 2).

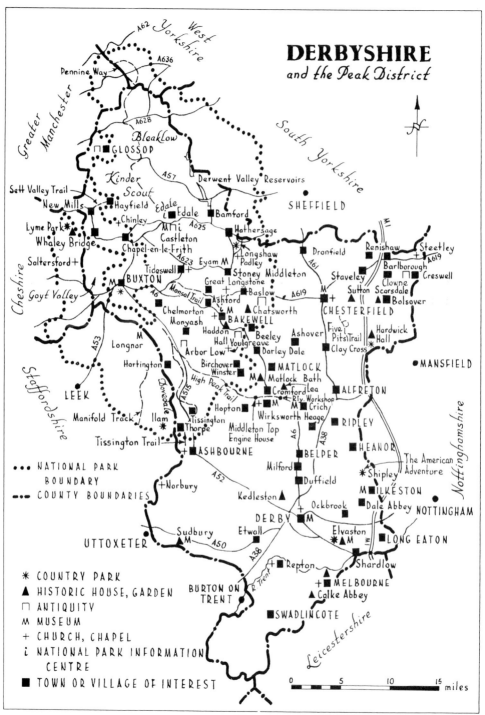

DERBYSHIRE
and the Peak District

West Yorkshire

A62

A636

Pennine Way

Greater Manchester

A628

Bleaklow

GLOSSOP

Kinder Scout

A57

Derwent Valley Reservoirs

South Yorkshire

SHEFFIELD

Sett Valley Trail

New Mills

Hayfield

Edale

Edale

Bamford

Lyme Park

Chinley

Hathersage

Whaley Bridge

Castleton

Dronfield

Renishaw

Steetley

A619

Chapel-en-le-Frith

A623

Eyam M

Longshaw Padley

Staveley

Barlborough

Creswell

Saltersford

A625

Clowne

Tideswell

Stoney Middleton

Sutton Scarsdale

Bolsover

Cheshire

BUXTON

Great Longstone

A6

Monsal Trail

Ashford

Baslow

A619

CHESTERFIELD

Goyt Valley

Chelmorton

Chatsworth

Five Pits Trail

Hardwick Hall

A53

Monyash

BAKEWELL

Ashover

Clay Cross

MANSFIELD

Longnor

Haddon Hall

Beeley

Youlgreave

Arbor Low

Darley Dale

Staffordshire

Hartington

Birchover

Winster

MATLOCK

Matlock Bath

Dovedale

High Peak Trail

Cromford Rly. Workshop

ALFRETON

LEEK

Hopton

Lea

Crich

Manifold Track

Ilam

A515

Middleton Top Engine House

Wirksworth Heage

RIPLEY

Tissington Trail

Thorpe

Tissington

HEANOR

••• NATIONAL PARK
    BOUNDARY

ASHBOURNE

Milford

BELPER

The American Adventure

–•– COUNTY BOUNDARIES

A52

Duffield

Shipley

Norbury

Kedleston

ILKESTON

Nottinghamshire

Ockbrook

Dale Abbey

NOTTINGHAM

Sudbury

Etwall

DERBY

Elvaston

LONG EATON

UTTOXETER

A450

A38

Repton

Shardlow

✳ COUNTRY PARK

Burton on Trent

R. Trent

MELBOURNE

▲ HISTORIC HOUSE, GARDEN

BURTON ON TRENT

Calke Abbey

☐ ANTIQUITY

M MUSEUM

SWADLINCOTE

Leicestershire

+ CHURCH, CHAPEL

i NATIONAL PARK INFORMATION
   CENTRE

■ TOWN OR VILLAGE OF INTEREST

0   5   10   15 miles

Index